CliffsNotes™

A Tale of Two Cities

By Marie Kalil

N THIS BOOK

- Discover Charles Dickens and his writing

- Preview an Introduction to the Novel

- Explore themes, character development, and recurring images in the Critical Commentaries

- Savor in-depth Character Analyses

- Understand the novel better through the Critical Essays

- Reinforce what you learn with CliffsNotes Review

- Find additional information to further your study in CliffsNotes Resource Center and online at www.cliffsnotes.com

D0596523

Wiley Publishing, Inc.

About the Author

Kris Marie Kalil received her M.A. from the University of Nebraska-Lincoln, specializing in nineteenth-century British and American literature. She has taught at the University of Nebraska at Omaha and Iowa Western Community College.

Publisher's Acknowledgments

Editorial

Project Editor: Kathleen M. Cox
Acquisitions Editor: Greg Tubach
Copy Editor: Corey Dalton
Glossary Editors: The editors and staff of Webster's New World Dictionaries
Editorial Assistant: Carol Strickland

Composition

Indexer: York Production Services, Inc.
Proofreader: York Production Services, Inc.
Wiley Publishing, Inc., Composition Services

CliffsNotes™ *A Tale of Two Cities*

Published by:
Wiley Publishing, Inc.
111 River St.
Hoboken, NJ 07030-5774
www.wiley.com
Copyright © 2000 Wiley Publishing, Inc., Hoboken, NJ
ISBN: 978-0-7645-8606-8
Printed in the United States of America
20 19 18 17 16 15
1O/RQ/QW/QS/IN
Published by Wiley Publishing, Inc., Hoboken, NJ
Published simultaneously in Canada

Library of Congress Cataloging-in-Publication Data
Kalil, Marie.
   CliffsNotes A Tale of Two Cities / by Marie Kalil.
      p.   cm.
   Includes bibliographical references and index.
   ISBN 978-0-7645-8606-4 (alk. paper)
   1. Dickens, Charles, 1812-1870. A Tale of Two Cities--Examinations--Study guides. 2. France--History-- Revolution, 1789-1799--Literature and the revolution. I. Title: Dickens' A Tale of Two Cities. II. Title: A Tale of Two Cities. III. Title.
PR4571 .K35 2000
823'.8--dc21   00–035107
                                              CIP

Table of Contents

ife and Background of the Author 1
Personal Background 2
Career Highlights 3

troduction to the Novel 6
Introduction 7
List of Characters 12
Character Map 15

ritical Commentaries 16

ook the First—Recalled to Life 17
Chapter 1—The Period 17
Chapter 2—The Mail 20
Chapter 3—The Night Shadows 22
Chapter 4—The Preparation 24
Chapter 5—The Wine-shop 26
Chapter 6—The Shoemaker 28

ook the Second—The Golden Thread 30
Chapter 1—Five Years Later 30
Chapter 2—A Sight 32
Chapter 3—A Disappointment 34
Chapter 4—Congratulatory 36
Chapter 5—The Jackal 38
Chapter 6—Hundreds of People 40
Chapter 7—Monseigneur in Town 42
Chapter 8—Monseigneur in the Country 44
Chapter 9—The Gorgon's Head 46
Chapter 10—Two Promises 47
Chapter 11—A Companion Picture 48
Chapter 12—The Fellow of Delicacy 49
Chapter 13—The Fellow of No Delicacy 50
Chapter 14—The Honest Tradesman 51
Chapter 15—Knitting 53
Chapter 16—Still Knitting 55
Chapter 17—One Night 57
Chapter 18—Nine Days 58
Chapter 19—An Opinion 59
Chapter 20—A Plea 61

Chapter 21—Echoing Footsteps 62
Chapter 22—The Sea Still Rises 64
Chapter 23—Fire Rises 66
Chapter 24—Drawn to the Loadstone Rock 67

Book the Third—The Track of a Storm **69**
Chapter 1—In Secret 69
Chapter 2—The Grindstone 71
Chapter 3—The Shadow 72
Chapter 4—Calm in Storm 74
Chapter 5—The Wood-Sawyer 76
Chapter 6—Triumph 77
Chapter 7—A Knock at the Door 78
Chapter 8—A Hand at Cards 79
Chapter 9—The Game Made 81
Chapter 10—The Substance of the Shadow 83
Chapter 11—Dusk 85
Chapter 12—Darkness 87
Chapter 13—Fifty-two 89
Chapter 14—The Knitting Done 91
Chapter 15—The Footsteps Die Out Forever 93

Character Analyses **95**
Doctor Alexandre Manette 96
Lucie Manette, later Darnay 96
Charles Darnay 97
Sydney Carton 97
Therese Defarge 98
Ernest Defarge 98
Jerry Cruncher 99

Critical Essays **101**
Women in *A Tale of Two Cities* 102
The French Revolution 103

CliffsNotes Review **109**
Q&A 109
Identify the Quote 110
Essay Questions 110
Practice Projects 111

CliffsNotes Resource Center **112**

Books and Articles 112

Internet 113

Recordings 114

Index **115**

How to Use This Book

This CliffsNotes study guide on Charles Dickens' *A Tale of Two Cities* supple ments the original literary work, giving you background information about th author, an introduction to the work, a graphical character map, critical commer taries, expanded glossaries, and a comprehensive index, all for you to use as an edu cational tool that will allow you to better understand *A Tale of Two Cities*. This stud guide was written with the assumption that you have read *A Tale of Two Cities*. Read ing a literary work doesn't mean that you immediately grasp the major themes an devices used by the author; this study guide will help supplement your reading t be sure you get all you can from Dickens' *A Tale of Two Cities*. CliffsNotes Revie tests your comprehension of the original text and reinforces learning with question and answers, practice projects, and more. For further information on Charles Dic ens and *A Tale of Two Cities*, check out the CliffsNotes Resource Center.

CliffsNotes provides the following icons to highlight essential elements of pa ticular interest:

Reveals the underlying themes in the work.

Helps you to more easily relate to or discover the depth of a character.

Uncovers elements such as setting, atmosphere, mystery, passion, violence, irony, symbolism, tragedy, foreshadowing, and satire.

Enables you to appreciate the nuances of words and phrases.

Don't Miss Our Web Site

Discover classic literature as well as modern-day treasures by visiting th CliffsNotes Web site at www.cliffsnotes.com. You can obtain a quick dow load of a CliffsNotes title, purchase a title in print form, browse our catalog, or vie online samples.

You'll also find interactive tools that are fun and informative, links to interestin Web sites, tips, articles, and additional resources to help you, not only for literatur but for test prep, finance, careers, computers, and Internet too. See you www.cliffsnotes.com!

LIFE AND BACKGROUND OF THE AUTHOR

The following abbreviated biography of Charles Dickens is provided so that you might become more familiar with his life and the historical times that possibly influenced his writing. Read this Life and Background of the Author section and recall it when reading Dickens' *A Tale of Two Cities*, thinking of any thematic relationship between Dickens' work and his life.

Personal Background 2

Career Highlights 3

Personal Background

Described as "the greatest English novelist," Charles Dickens is studied more than any other author writing in English, except for Shakespeare. While his popularity with critics has fluctuated over time, Dickens' works have never lost their appeal for general readers, thanks to the universality of his writing. He infused his realistic depictions of society and memorable characters with enough humor and sensitivity to entertain and satisfy both casual and serious readers.

Charles Dickens was born in Portsmouth, Hampshire, on February 7, 1812, to John and Elizabeth Barrow Dickens. His family moved several times during his early years and finally settled in Chatham, a seaport town in southern England, from 1817 to 1822. The Chatham years were happy ones for Dickens; he attended a good school and found much in the busy town and open countryside to entertain his active mind.

In 1822, Dickens' father's job transferred the family to London, where financial problems eventually led to John Dickens being sent to debtor's prison in 1824. Although the rest of his family joined his father in prison, twelve-year-old Charles lived alone and worked at Warren's Blacking Factory. Although the experience lasted for only a few months, it affected him deeply. Images of orphaned children and prisons would permeate his stories and books throughout his writing career.

After being removed from the factory, Dickens spent the next three years attending the Wellington House Academy, where he won a Latin prize. At the age of fifteen, he left school and began working as a solicitor's clerk at the law firm of Ellis and Blackmore. He eventually became a shorthand reporter in the Doctors' Commons law courts and then a parliamentary and news reporter for the *Morning Chronicle* newspaper. His years of observing the legal system gave him a familiarity and contempt for the law and politics, which his books echo.

After an unsuccessful courtship of Maria Beadnell, a banker's daughter whose parents viewed Dickens' family and prospects as inadequate, Dickens turned his attentions to Catherine Hogarth, daughter of journalist George Hogarth. Dickens and Catherine married on April 2, 1836, and eventually had ten children: Charles, Mary, Kate, Walter, Francis, Alfred, Sydney, Henry, Dora, and Edward.

Domestically, Dickens eventually became estranged from his wife. The couple separated in 1858, and Dickens began a relationship with actress Ellen Ternan that would last for the rest of his life. In March 1870, exhausted by his hectic schedule of readings and appearances, Dickens gave his last public reading, stating, "From these garish lights I vanish now for evermore." Three months later, on June 9, 1870, Dickens died at age fifty-eight from a stroke and was buried in the Poet's Corner of Westminster Abbey. He remains one of England's most popular authors, and readers throughout the world continue to enjoy his books and stories.

Career Highlights

In 1833, Dickens started publishing "sketches," or brief, informal stories and essays, in the *Monthly Magazine* and in the *Morning Chronicle* under the pseudonym "Boz." In February 1836, a collection of his sketches appeared as *Sketches by Boz*. Also in February, Dickens received a contract to write his first novel, a series of 20 monthly installments called *The Pickwick Papers*. The popularity of the story of Samuel Pickwick and his Pickwick Club increased with each installment; by the last chapter, the number of copies being sold had grown from 1,000 to 40,000, an exceptional number for the time.

The success of *The Pickwick Papers* launched a new era in publishing. The concept of publishing a novel in installments was a new one at the time, but it soon caught on with other authors, including Anthony Trollope, William Makepeace Thackeray, and Wilkie Collins. Serial literature benefited the publisher, the reader, and the author through its affordability and accessibility. Publishers could introduce a new title for one-twentieth the cost of publishing an entire book, plus the advantage of selling advertising space in the publication. Meanwhile, readers gained a cheap source of literature and authors received payment for each installment, rather than waiting for the entire book to be finished before they could sell it and be paid. Writing in installments worked well for Dickens, and he used this method to publish all of his major fiction.

From 1837 to 1838, Dickens continued his literary success with *Oliver Twist*, a story of an orphan boy's experiences with the criminal world of London. He followed that with *Nicholas Nickleby* (1838-39), which exposed the abusive nature of Yorkshire boarding schools and narrated the humorous adventures of a traveling theater company. Victorian audiences made his next book, *The Old Curiosity Shop* (1840-41), phenomenally popular—the morality tale of Little Nell roaming the countryside with her mad grandfather as they try to evade the malicious Daniel Quilp enthralled readers and sold over 100,000 copies a week.

However, the Victorian audience did not take to Dickens' next two books, *Barnaby Rudge* (1841) and *Martin Chuzzlewit* (1843-44). Dickens' first historical novel, *Barnaby Rudge* dealt with the Gordon Riots that occurred in England in 1780, and its poorly structured story resulted in a steady drop in sales. In *Martin Chuzzlewit*, Dickens returned to Victorian England as a setting and used the materialism of the Chuzzlewit family to highlight a theme of selfishness. *Martin Chuzzlewit* received mixed reviews and sales that improved slightly throughout the course of its publication.

Technically superior to Dickens' earlier works, with a more cohesive plot and characters, *Dombey and Son* (1846-48) signals the beginning of Dickens' more mature works. The novel explores the theme of pride through the story of the Dombeys, a family of wealthy merchants. Dickens followed *Dombey and Son* with *David Copperfield* (1849-50), an autobiographical novel that examines Copperfield's early hardship and later rise to prominence through a first-person narrative.

Continuing to build upon his skills, Dickens was not afraid to experiment in his novels. In *Bleak House* (1852-53), his satire of the chancery courts and examination of Victorian society, Dickens uses both a third-person narrative and a first-person narrator to connect the societal perspective with a personal one. In his shortest book, *Hard Times* (1854), Dickens highlights industrial and educational issues through a moral fable. Meanwhile, scholars consider Dickens' eleventh novel, *Little Dorrit* (1855-57), to be one of his most difficult novels. It presents a view of society as a series of prisons, focusing especially on the oppressive natures of class privilege and religion.

Remarkably, even as Dickens became a master of his craft and enjoyed critical and popular success, he never stopped trying new approaches to telling a story. His second historical novel, *A Tale of Two Cities* (1859), recounts the events of the French Revolution. In it, he experimented with developing the characters through the action of the plot rather than through dialogue and detailed description.

His next book, *Great Expectations* (1860-61), focuses on the theme of corruption and follows the first-person narrative of Pip, a young man trying to become a gentleman. Unlike *David Copperfield*, *Great Expectations* examines the coming-of-age process with irony and social insight. Dickens' last completed novel, *Our Mutual Friend* (1864-65), deals with the corrupting power of money and the superficiality of society through a third-person narrative. His final novel, *The Mystery of Edwin Drood* (1870), was left unfinished. Critics continue to debate whether the story was intended to be a study in the psychology of its characters or a murder mystery thriller.

Dickens' novels are his outstanding achievement, but he also wrote nonfiction articles, two travel books, Christmas stories, and a history of England for children. Additionally, as he steadily wrote novels, Dickens continued his journalistic career, working as an editor at the periodicals *Bentley's Miscellany* and *Master Humphrey's Clock*.

INTRODUCTION TO THE NOVEL

The following Introduction section is provided solely as an educational tool and is not meant to replace the experience of your reading the work. Read the Introduction and A Brief Synopsis to enhance your understanding of the work and to prepare yourself for the critical thinking that should take place whenever you read any work of fiction or nonfiction. Keep the List of Characters and Character Map at hand so that as you read the original literary work, if you encounter a character about whom you're uncertain, you can refer to the List of Characters and Character Map to refresh your memory.

Introduction **7**

List of Characters **12**

Character Map **15**

Introduction

Scholars describe *A Tale of Two Cities* as the least Dickensian of Dickens' novels, yet it remains one of Dickens' most widely read books. It was originally published in weekly installments in *All the Year Round,* from April 30 to November 29, 1859. From the book's inception, it received mixed critical reviews, but succeeded in capturing the imagination of general readers through its swift, exciting story and memorable rendering of the French Revolution.

The idea for *A Tale of Two Cities* originated in two main sources. Always interested in the interaction between individuals and society, Dickens was particularly intrigued by Thomas Carlyle's history, *The French Revolution.* He saw similarities between the forces that led to the Revolution and the oppression and unrest occurring in England in his own time. Although he supported the idea of people rising up against tyranny, the violence that characterized the French Revolution troubled him.

Dickens was also drawn to the themes inherent in *The Frozen Deep,* a play that Wilkie Collins wrote and in which Dickens acted. In the play, two men compete for the same woman, Clara Burnham. When she chooses Frank Aldersley over Richard Wardour, Wardour (played by Dickens) vows revenge upon his rival, even though he doesn't know who his rival is. While on an arctic expedition together, the two men get stranded. Wardour discovers that Aldersley is his rival, but instead of leaving him to die, Wardour overcomes his anger and saves Aldersley's life by carrying him to safety. Collapsing at Clara's feet, Wardour dies from his efforts while Clara weeps over him. The idea of Wardour's heroism and sacrifice strongly affected Dickens, and during the course of the play, as Dickens notes in the preface to *A Tale of Two Cities,* he "conceived the main idea of this story."

An examination of Dickens' personal life at the time he decided to write *A Tale of Two Cities* also reveals what may have motivated him to write this particular story. His marriage to Catherine Hogarth had been deteriorating for years, and in May 1858, they decided to separate. Meanwhile, he had met a young woman named Ellen Ternan while performing in *The Frozen Deep,* and began a clandestine relationship with her that would continue until his death. Additionally, a disagreement with his publishers at *Household Words* led to his resignation as editor and the creation of a new magazine, *All the Year Round.* Dickens used *A Tale of Two Cities* to launch the new magazine, and the themes of secrecy and upheaval that run throughout the book may be reflections of the experiences Dickens was encountering in his own life.

Dickens took a different approach to writing *A Tale of Two Cities* than to his previous novels and described the book as an experiment. Rather than relying upon dialogue to develop characters, Dickens instead relied upon the plot. Consequently, the characters are defined by their actions and by their place within the movement of the overall story. Critics have complained that this technique results in a loss of Dickens' strengths in his writing, including his sense of humor and his memorable characters. They agree, however, that Dickens' experiment created his most tightly plotted novel, in which the narrative moves along quickly and smoothly. The book's well-conceived structure neatly blends all of the storylines and characters, so that by the end of the book, no question remains as to how each element of the book impacts all the others.

Dickens' social ideas in this novel are straightforward: the French Revolution was inevitable because the aristocracy exploited and plundered the poor, driving them to revolt. Therefore, oppression on a large scale results in anarchy, and anarchy produces a police state. One of Dickens' strongest convictions was that the English people might erupt at any moment into a mass of bloody revolutionists. It is clear today that he was mistaken, but the idea was firmly planted in his mind, as well as in the minds of his contemporaries. *A Tale of Two Cities* was partly an attempt to show his readers the dangers of a possible revolution. This idea was not the first time a simple—and incorrect—conviction became the occasion for a serious and powerful work of art.

Violent revolutionary activity caught up almost all of Europe during the first half of the nineteenth century, and middle-class Englishmen naturally feared that widespread rebellion might take place at home. Dickens knew what poverty was like and how common it was. He realized the inadequacy of philanthropic institutions when confronted by the enormous misery of the slums. That Dickens turned to the French Revolution to dramatize the possibility of class uprisings is not surprising; few events in history offer such a concentration of terrors.

If the terrors of the French Revolution take a political form, the hope that Dickens holds out in this novel has distinct religious qualities. On a basic level, *A Tale of Two Cities* is a fable about resurrection, depicting the main characters, Doctor Manette, Charles Darnay, and Sydney Carton, as all being "recalled to life" in different ways. The Doctor regains his freedom and sanity, Darnay escapes a death sentence three times, and Carton redeems his soul through sacrifice. By using the theme of resurrection, Dickens demonstrates that the spiritual lives of all people depend upon the hope of renewal. Without such hope, as in the case of Madame Defarge, people lose what makes them human and resort to violence and cruelty.

In order to convey the significance of revolution and resurrection in the novel, Dickens relied upon his descriptive skills, which are perhaps at their best in *A Tale of Two Cities*. Dickens adeptly portrays the horrors of mob violence throughout the novel, leaving the reader with images of waves of people crashing through the battered gates of the Bastille; of Foulon with his mouth stuffed full of grass as he is beaten to death and beheaded; of the hundreds of unruly citizens singing and dancing wildly around Lucie Manette as she stands alone outside her husband's prison. However, Dickens balances these visions of revolutionary terror with images of rebirth and hope, such as Lucie's golden hair mingling with her father's prematurely white hair in the moments after he first remembers her mother, and Carton's prophetic vision of the future as he goes to the guillotine. Although *A Tale of Two Cities* lacks the wealth of memorable characters found in other Dickens novels, the unforgettable images Dickens creates compensate for this deficiency.

In the latter half of the twentieth century, critics began to reexamine previous assessments of *A Tale of Two Cities* based on new trends in criticism. Biographical critics read the book in terms of the revolution occurring in Dickens' life, while psychological critics analyzed the relationships between fathers and sons and the prison imagery in terms of Dickens' childhood. Meanwhile, historical and Marxist critics examined *A Tale of Two Cities* as a work of historical fiction and in terms of political overtones. Although few people champion the book as the best of Dickens' novels, critics have given it more respect and increased attention in recent decades.

Regardless of critical interest in the novel, theatrical and film interpretations of *A Tale of Two Cities* have fascinated audiences since Dickens first published the book. Various productions have retold the story of Carton's sacrifice, including one in which John Barsad saves Carton from the guillotine. The tale was especially popular with early moviegoers; five silent films of the book were made between 1908 and 1925. Since then, two more films of *A Tale of Two Cities* were made in 1935 and 1957, and the story has been repeatedly adapted for radio and television. Such frequent interpretation by the media, combined with the large number of students who read the novel each year, demonstrates that Dickens' story of revolution, sacrifice, and redemption continues to captivate modern imaginations.

A Brief Synopsis

"It was the best of times, it was the worst of times," Dickens writes in the opening lines of *A Tale of Two Cities* as he paints a picture of life in England and France. The year is late 1775, and Jarvis Lorry travels from London to Paris on a secret mission for his employer, Tellson's Bank. Joining him on his journey is Lucie Manette, a 17-year-old woman who is stunned to learn that her father, Doctor Alexandre Manette, is alive and has recently been released after having been secretly imprisoned in Paris for 18 years.

When Mr. Lorry and Lucie arrive in Paris, they find the Doctor's former servant, Ernest Defarge, caring for the him. Defarge now runs a wine-shop with his wife in the poverty-stricken quarter of Saint Antoine. Defarge takes Mr. Lorry and Lucie to the garret room where he is keeping Doctor Manette, warning them that the Doctor's years in prison have greatly changed him. Thin and pale, Doctor Manette sits at a shoemaker's bench intently making shoes. He barely responds to questions from Defarge and Mr. Lorry, but when Lucie approaches him, he remembers his wife and begins to weep. Lucie comforts him, and that night Mr. Lorry and Lucie take him to England.

Five years later, the porter for Tellson's Bank, Jerry Cruncher, takes a message to Mr. Lorry who is at a courthouse. Mr. Lorry has been called as a witness for the trial of Charles Darnay, a Frenchman accused of being a spy for France and the United States. Also at the trial are Doctor Manette and Lucie, who are witnesses for the prosecution. Doctor Manette has fully recovered and has formed a close bond with his daughter.

If found guilty of treason, Darnay will suffer a gruesome death, and the testimony of an acquaintance, John Barsad, and a former servant, Roger Cly, seems sure to result in a guilty verdict. Questions from Darnay's attorney, Mr. Stryver, indicate that Cly and Barsad are the real spies, but the turning point in the trial occurs when Sydney Carton, Stryver's assistant, points out that Carton and Darnay look alike enough to be doubles. This revelation throws into doubt a positive identification of Darnay as the person seen passing secrets, and the court acquits Darnay.

After the trial, Darnay, Carton, and Stryver begin spending time at the Manette home, obviously attracted to Lucie's beauty and kind nature. Stryver decides to propose to her, but is dissuaded by Mr. Lorry. Carton confesses his love to Lucie, but does not propose, knowing that his drunken and apathetic way of life is not worthy of her. However, he vows that he would gladly give his life to save a life she loved, and Lucie is moved by his sincerity and devotion. Eventually, it is Darnay whose love Lucie returns, and the two marry with Doctor Manette's uneasy blessing. While the couple is on their honeymoon, the Doctor suffers a nine-day relapse of his mental incapacity and believes he is making shoes in prison again.

Meanwhile, the situation in France grows worse. Signs of unrest become evident when Darnay's cruel and unfeeling uncle, the Marquis St. Evrémonde, is murdered in his bed after running down a child with his carriage in the Paris streets. Although Darnay inherits the title and the estate, he has renounced all ties to his brutal family and works instead in England as a tutor of French language and literature.

The Revolution erupts with full force in July 1789 with the storming of the Bastille. The Defarges are at the center of the revolutionary movement and lead the people in a wave of violence and destruction. By 1792, the revolutionaries have taken control of France and are imprisoning and killing anyone they view as an enemy of the state. Darnay receives a letter from the Evrémonde steward, who has been captured and who begs Darnay to come to France to save him. Feeling a sense of duty to his servant and not fully realizing the danger awaiting him, Darnay departs for France. Once he reaches Paris, though, revolutionaries take him to La Force prison "in secret," with no way of contacting anyone and with little hope of a trial.

Doctor Manette, Lucie, and Lucie's daughter soon arrive in Paris and join Mr. Lorry who is at Tellson's Paris office. Doctor Manette's status as a former prisoner of the Bastille gives him a heroic status with the revolutionaries and enables him to find out what has happened to his son-in-law. He uses his influence to get a trial for Darnay, and Doctor Manette's powerful testimony at the trial frees his son-in-law. Hours after being reunited with his wife and daughter, however, the revolutionaries again arrest Darnay, based on the accusations of the Defarges.

The next day, Darnay is tried again. This time, the Defarges produce a letter written years earlier by Doctor Manette in prison condemning all Evrémondes for the murder of Madame Defarge's family and for imprisoning the Doctor. Based on this evidence, the court sentences Darnay to death and Doctor Manette, devastated by what has happened, reverts to his prior state of dementia.

Unknown to the Manette and Darnay family, Sydney Carton has arrived in Paris and learns of Darnay's fate. He also hears of a plot contrived to send Lucie and her daughter to the guillotine. Determined to save their lives, he enlists the help of a prison spy to enter the prison where the revolutionaries are holding Darnay. He enters Darnay's cell, changes clothes with him, drugs him, and has Darnay taken out of the prison in his place. No one questions either man's identity because of the similarities in their features. As Mr. Lorry shepherds Doctor Manette, Darnay, Lucie, and young Lucie out of France, Carton goes to the guillotine, strengthened and comforted by the knowledge that his sacrifice has saved the woman he loves and her family.

List of Characters

Doctor Alexandre Manette A doctor from Beauvais, France, who was secretly imprisoned in the Bastille for 18 years and suffers some mental trauma from the experience. After being released, he is nursed back to health by his daughter, Lucie, in England. During the Revolution, he tries to save his son-in-law, Charles Darnay, from the guillotine.

Lucie Manette, later Darnay A beautiful young woman recognized for her kindness and compassion. After being reunited with her father, she cares for him and remains devoted to him, even after her marriage to Charles Darnay.

Charles Darnay A French aristocrat. Darnay renounces his family name of St. Evrémonde and moves to England, where he works as a tutor and eventually marries Lucie Manette. He is put on trial during the Revolution for the crimes of his family.

Sydney Carton A lawyer who looks like Charles Darnay and who lives in a fog of apathy and alcohol. His love for Lucie Manette motivates him to sacrifice his life to save the life of her husband.

Mr. Jarvis Lorry An English banker. A loyal friend to the Manette family, Mr. Lorry shepherds the family out of Paris after the Doctor's release from prison and during the Revolution.

Ernest Defarge The owner of a wine-shop in a Paris suburb. Defarge is a leader of the Jacquerie (a roving band of peasants) during the French Revolution.

Madame Thérèse Defarge A hard, vengeful woman who is married to Ernest Defarge. Madame Defarge knits a registry with the names of aristocrats she condemns and later leads the female revolutionaries in killing and exacting revenge on her enemies.

Miss Pross A forceful Englishwoman who was Lucie Manette's nursemaid. She remains Lucie's devoted servant and protector.

Jerry Cruncher A messenger for Tellson's Bank and Jarvis Lorry's bodyguard. He is also secretly a graverobber.

Mrs. Cruncher Jerry's wife. A pious woman, she is frequently beaten by her husband for praying.

Young Jerry Cruncher Jerry's son, who resembles his father in appearance and temperament. He assists Jerry at Tellson's.

C. J. Stryver A boorish lawyer who employs Sydney Carton. Stryver is Darnay's defense attorney in England and aspires briefly to marry Lucie.

Roger Cly A police spy in England who faked his own funeral. He appears later as a prison spy in revolutionary France.

John Barsad, or Solomon Pross A police spy in England who becomes a spy in revolutionary France. Recognized as Miss Pross' brother, he is forced to help Carton save Darnay.

Monseigneur the Marquis A greedy, self-absorbed French aristocrat. He personifies all that is wrong with the upper classes in pre-Revolutionary France.

Marquis St. Evrémonde   Darnay's uncle. An immoral, cruel man, he runs down a child with his carriage and is later murdered by the child's father.

Jacques One, Two, Three, and Four   Members of the Jacquerie, the revolutionaries who organize and implement the French Revolution. The name comes from the nickname for peasants.

Théophile Gabelle   An agent for the St. Evrémonde family. The revolutionaries imprison this man during the Revolution for handling some business affairs for Darnay. His letter begging for help sends Darnay back to France.

Gaspard   A peasant. This man murders the Marquis St. Evrémonde for running down and killing his child.

Road-mender and Wood-sawyer   A peasant. This man becomes a bloodthirsty revolutionist.

Young Lucie Darnay   The daughter of Lucie and Charles Darnay. Madame Defarge threatens her life during the Reign of Terror.

Foulon   A callous prison official who faked his own death. He is hanged and decapitated by a mob after they storm the Bastille.

The Vengeance   The grocer's wife. Turned vicious by the Revolution, she becomes Madame Defarge's main companion.

A Seamstress   A frightened young woman who is executed with Carton. She and Carton comfort each other on the way to the guillotine.

Character Map

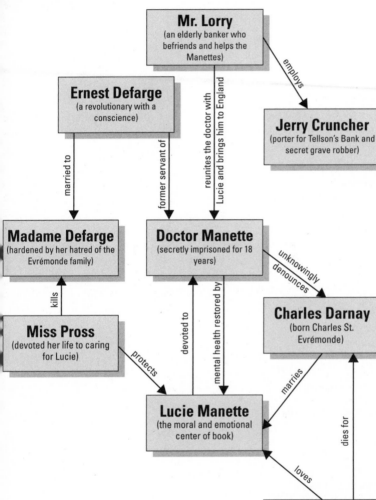

Mr. Lorry
(an elderly banker who befriends and helps the Manettes)

employs

Jerry Cruncher
(porter for Tellson's Bank and secret grave robber)

Ernest Defarge
(a revolutionary with a conscience)

reunites the doctor with Lucie and brings him to England

married to

former servant of

Madame Defarge
(hardened by her hatred of the Evrémonde family)

Doctor Manette
(secretly imprisoned for 18 years)

unknowingly denounces

kills

devoted to

mental health restored by

Charles Darnay
(born Charles St. Evrémonde)

Miss Pross
(devoted her life to caring for Lucie)

protects

Lucie Manette
(the moral and emotional center of book)

marries

dies for

loves

Sidney Carton
(an alcoholic lawyer who finds redemption through his death)

CRITICAL COMMENTARIES

The sections that follow provide great tools for supplementing your reading of *A Tale of Two Cities*. First, in order to enhance your understanding of and enjoyment from reading, we provide quick summaries in case you have difficulty when you read the original literary work. Each summary is followed by commentary: literary devices, character analyses, themes, and so on. Keep in mind that the interpretations here are solely those of the author of this study guide and are used to jumpstart your thinking about the work. No single interpretation of a complex work like *A Tale of Two Cities* is infallible or exhaustive, and you'll likely find that you interpret portions of the work differently from the author of this study guide. Read the original work and determine your own interpretations, referring to these Notes for supplemental meanings only.

Book the First 17

Chapter 1 — The Period 17

Chapter 2—The Mail 20

Chapter 3—The Night
Shadows 22

Chapter 4—The
Preparation 24

Chapter 5—The
Wine-shop 26

Chapter 6—The
Shoemaker 28

Book the Second 30

Chapter 1 — Five
Years Later 30

Chapter 2—A Sight 32

Chapter 3—A
Disappointment 34

Chapter 4—
Congratulatory 36

Chapter 5—The Jackal 38

Chapter 6—Hundreds of
People 40

Chapter 7—Monseigneur
in Town 42

Chapter 8—Monseigneur
in the Country 44

Chapter 9—The
Gorgon's Head 46

Chapter 10—Two
Promises 47

Chapter 11—A Companion
Picture 48

Chapter 12—The Fellow of
Delicacy 49

Chapter 13—The Fellow
of No Delicacy 50

Chapter 14—The Honest
Tradesman 51

Chapter 15—Knitting 53

Chapter 16—Still Knitting . . . 55

Chapter 17—One Night 57

Chapter 18—Nine Days 58

Chapter 19—An Opinion 59

Chapter 20—A Plea 61

Chapter 21—Echoing
Footsteps 62

Chapter 22—The Sea Still
Rises 64

Chapter 23—Fire Rises 66

Chapter 24—Drawn to the
Loadstone Rock 67

Book the Third 69

Chapter 1—In Secret 69

Chapter 2 —The
Grindstone 71

Chapter 3—The Shadow 72

Chapter 4 —Calm in
Storm 74

Chapter 5—The Wood-
Sawyer 76

Chapter 6—Triumph 77

Chapter 7—A Knock at
the Door 78

Chapter 8—A Hand
at Cards 79

Chapter 9—The Game
Made 81

Chapter 10—The Substance
of the Shadow 83

Chapter 11—Dusk 85

Chapter 12—Darkness 87

Chapter 13—Fifty-two 89

Chapter 14—The
Knitting Done 91

Chapter 15—The Footsteps
Die Out Forever 93

Book the First—Recalled to Life
Chapter 1—The Period

Summary

The year is 1775, and life in England and France seems paradoxically the best and the worst that it can be. The rulers and ruling classes of both countries may have the best of life, but they are out of touch with the common people and believe that the status quo will continue forever.

In France, inflation is out of control and an oppressive social system results in intolerable and extreme injustices being committed against average citizens, who believe they have the worst of life. The breaking point—riotous rebellion—is near, and the populace of France secretly but steadily moves toward revolution.

Meanwhile, in England, people give spiritualists and the supernatural more attention than the revolutionary rumblings from American colonists, and an ineffective justice system leads to widespread violence and crime. While the English and French kings and queens carelessly ignore the unrest and misery prevalent in their countries, silent forces guide the rulers and their people toward fate and death.

Commentary

Theme

This first chapter presents the sweeping backdrop of forces and events that will shape the lives of the novel's characters. From the first paragraph, Dickens begins developing the central theme of duality. His pairings of contrasting concepts such as the "best" and "worst" of times, "Light" and "Darkness," and "hope" and "despair" reflect the mirror images of good and evil that will recur in characters and situations throughout the novel.

England and France in 1775 embody the concept of duality that Dickens outlines in the first paragraph. Both countries are simultaneously experiencing very similar and very different situations. For example, both the English and French monarchs—George III and Louis

XVI, respectively—seem indifferent to the plight of their people and cannot comprehend any power being great enough to eclipse their divine right to rule. However, while their attitudes will result in revolutions for both countries, the American revolution occurs an ocean away, leaving the British infrastructure unscathed and saving the British population from the massive loss of life and the horrors that will take place during the French Revolution.

The differences between the two countries become more pronounced when Dickens compares the concepts of spirituality and justice in each country. In England, people are enthralled with the supernatural, especially with visionaries and ghosts that communicate mystical messages. In France, though, people pay attention to religious leaders out of fear rather than fascination. A man neglecting to kneel to a distant procession of monks may be condemned to a torturous death for his transgression. Dickens contrasts France's harsh justice system to England's lax one. Criminals overrun England: Highwaymen rob seemingly at will, prisoners revolt against their jailers, and violence is answered with more violence. When the courts serve justice in England, they serve it indiscriminately, with murderers and petty thieves alike receiving the death penalty.

Glossary

(Here and in the following sections, difficult words and phrases are explained.)

a king with a large jaw and a queen with a plain face on the throne of England King George III and Queen Charlotte Sophia.

a king with a large jaw and a queen with a fair face on the throne of France King Louis XVI and Queen Marie Antoinette.

Mrs. Southcott Joanna Southcott (1750-1814), an English religious visionary.

Cock-lane ghost a poltergeist phenomenon studied by Horace Walpole, Dr. Johnson, and Oliver Goldsmith. People greatly debated its authenticity.

"a congress of British subjects in America" In January 1775, the American Continental Congress presented a petition of its grievances to the British Parliament.

a certain movable framework that is, the guillotine.

highwayman a man, especially one on horseback, who robbed travelers on a highway.

stand and deliver a highwayman's order to his victims to stand still and deliver their money and valuables.

gaols British spelling of jails.

turnkey a person in charge of the keys of a prison; warder; jailer.

blunderbusses muskets with a large bore and a broad, flaring muzzle, accurate only at close range.

Newgate a London prison notorious for its inhumane conditions.

Westminster Hall Westminster Hall, located in London, was the chief law court of England until 1870.

Chapter 2—The Mail

Summary

In England, the Dover mail coach makes its way up a hill one late November night. The foreboding atmosphere of night and mist makes everyone uneasy—the passengers, the coachman, and the guard. Highway robberies are common, and the travelers are as wary of each other as they are of anyone else they might meet on the road.

As the coach reaches the top of the hill, the travelers hear a horse approaching at a gallop. The rider, Jerry, is a messenger from Tellson's Bank in London, and he has a message for one of the passengers, Mr. Jarvis Lorry, an employee of the bank. Mr. Lorry reads the message, which states, "Wait at Dover for Mam'selle." Mr. Lorry tells Jerry to return the answer, "Recalled to Life," and the coach continues on its way. As Jerry gallops back to London, he muses over Mr. Lorry's mysterious response.

Commentary

Like many nineteenth-century authors, Dickens uses atmosphere and setting to establish the mood of a story, and this chapter exemplifies his mastery of the technique. The action of the novel begins with discomfort and anxiety as the characters slog along the muddy highway in the dark, damp chill of a late November mist. The threat of highway robbery that Dickens describes in the first chapter combines with the misty cold to create a sense of vulnerability and apprehension.

Mr. Lorry serves as a figurative and actual link between France and England throughout the book. As Dickens reveals in later chapters, Mr. Lorry is first and foremost a man of business, and his business—Tellson's Bank—carries him between England and France. At this point, though, his current business is a mystery to everyone but himself.

The messages exchanged between him and Jerry are a puzzle to all that hear them, especially Mr. Lorry's response: "Recalled to life." This theme of mystery and secrecy will recur repeatedly and will play a central role in the unfolding of the plot.

Glossary

the mail short for "mail coach," a coach that carried mail and passengers.

arm-chest a chest containing weapons.

cutlass a short, curving sword, originally used by sailors.

jack-boots heavy, sturdy military boots that extend above the knees.

"The rider's horse was blown" The horse was out of breath.

flint and steel Flint is a fine-grained, very hard rock that produces sparks when struck against a piece of steel. Before the invention of matches, people used flint and steel to start fires.

Chapter 3—The Night Shadows

Summary

As the coach rattles its way toward Dover, Mr. Lorry dozes restlessly, reflecting upon his mission, "to dig some one out of a grave" who has been "buried alive for eighteen years." He envisions what the face of the man must look like and contemplates how severely the years may have affected him. Haunted by visions of the man's face, Mr. Lorry imagines a dialogue in which he repeatedly asks the man, "I hope you care to live?" and the man always responds, "I can't say."

Commentary

Literary Device

Continuing the theme of secrecy, Dickens compares Mr. Lorry's secret to the inner lives of all people, stating that every person is a "profound secret and mystery to every other." Dickens uses the passengers in the coach to demonstrate his point: Although the three men are traveling a long distance together in very close quarters, they act solitary enough to be traveling alone. Additionally, as described in Chapter 2, the passengers are so bundled up against the cold that distinguishing any of their features is impossible. Their physical anonymity, combined with their mistrust of each other due to the prevalence of robberies, causes the three passengers to completely isolate themselves from one another. This concept of mystery and isolation becomes increasingly important as the book progresses and characters begin to make decisions based upon close-kept secrets.

Theme

Also important in this chapter is the introduction of the resurrection theme. Someone is indeed going to be "recalled to life," and the questions raised by such an event haunt Mr. Lorry. "Recalled to Life" is also the title of Book I of *A Tale of Two Cities*, which indicates that the upcoming resurrection is vital to the development of the plot in this section of the novel. Although you still don't know who the "dead" man is or from where he is being resurrected, you do know that he is somehow central to the plot.

Dickens symbolically represents the significance of the resurrection at the end of the chapter when Mr. Lorry awakens at daybreak and looks out the coach window at a partially ploughed field, a wood, and the sun rising into the clear sky. His troubled dreams have been dissolved by the sunrise—a rebirth or resurrection of the sun—and the sun rises to illuminate a field and a wood—the provinces of Death (the farmer) and Fate (the woodman) that Dickens introduced in the first chapter. With this imagery, Dickens suggests that recalling the mystery man to life will also bring to light the silent forces that are moving France toward revolution.

Glossary

"Something of the awfulness" Something of the impressiveness. "Awfulness" here means "inspiring awe" rather than "terrible."

coach and six a coach drawn by six horses.

alehouse a place where ale is sold and served; tavern.

cocked-hat a three-cornered hat with a turned-up brim.

Chapter 4—The Preparation

Summary

Mr. Lorry arrives at the Royal George Hotel in Dover in the late morning. After freshening up, he spends the day relaxing and meditating on his mission while he waits for the young woman, Lucie Manette, to arrive. When Lucie arrives, Mr. Lorry introduces himself and proceeds to divulge the nature of her involvement in his current business in Paris. Apparently Lucie's father, Doctor Manette, whom she believed to be dead, is alive, and has been secretly imprisoned in Paris for the past eighteen years. The French authorities have recently released Doctor Manette, and Tellson's Bank is sending Mr. Lorry to identify the Doctor (who was one of Tellson's clients) and bring him to the safety of England. As the Doctor's daughter, Lucie will be responsible for caring for him and nursing him back to health. The story shocks Lucie; when Mr. Lorry tries to comfort her, she simply stares at him, gripping his arm. Concerned by her numbed state, Mr. Lorry calls for help. A large, red-haired woman runs into the room, shoves Mr. Lorry away from Lucie and into a wall, and begins yelling at the inn's servants to bring smelling salts and cold water.

Commentary

As Mr. Lorry emerges from his room at the Royal George, the curious servants hover nearby to see what he looks like after shedding his bulky winter coat and hat. Similarly, Dickens' readers also wait for Dickens to reveal Mr. Lorry and his secret. As Dickens fills in the physical details of Mr. Lorry's person, he is signifying that the details of Mr. Lorry's character and his mission will also soon be revealed.

Character Insight

What you discover is that, although Mr. Lorry insists that he is simply a man of business with no more feelings than a machine, he is actually a kind man who is deeply troubled by the Manettes' situation. His concern is apparent in his dreams about digging out Doctor Manette and in the gentle way in which he discloses to Lucie that her father is alive; he initially presents her father's story as the story of an anonymous customer to give her time to adjust to the shocking news. Notice however, that although Mr. Lorry's mission is no longer a secret, the resolution to one mystery leads to another—why was Doctor Manette secretly imprisoned?

Glossary

forenoon morning; the part of the day before noon.

drawer a bartender; tapster.

packet a boat that travels a regular route, as along a coast or river, carrying passengers, mail, and freight.

Calais a seaport in northern France, on the Strait of Dover; located across the English Channel from Dover.

claret a dry, red wine, especially red Bordeaux.

linen things made of linen; in this case, shirts.

piscatory flavor a fishy flavor.

horsehair a stiff fabric made from the hair of the mane or tail of a horse.

Channel the English Channel.

pier glass a tall mirror set on a pier, or wall section, between two windows.

Beauvais a town in France north of Paris.

pecuniary of or involving money.

compatriot a fellow countryman.

"the privilege of filling up blank forms" members of the French aristocracy could issue warrants for the indefinite imprisonment of their enemies without a trial.

Grenadier wooden measure a tall, cylindrical measuring cup.

smelling salts an aromatic mixture of carbonate of ammonium and some fragrant scent used as an inhalant in relieving faintness, headaches, and the like.

Chapter 5—The Wine-shop

Summary

A street in the Parisian suburb of Saint Antoine is the scene of chaos as a crowd gathers in front of a wine-shop to scoop up pools of wine spilled from a broken cask. When the wine is gone, the people resume their everyday activities. Left behind, however, are the stains of the red wine on the street and the people's hands, faces, and feet, foreshadowing the blood that will be spilled there in later years.

Inside the wine-shop, Monsieur and Madame Defarge converse with three other men, all called "Jacques." Monsieur Defarge sends the men upstairs, to a chamber on the fifth floor. Meanwhile, Mr. Lorry and Lucie have entered the shop and, after a brief discussion with Monsieur Defarge, they follow him upstairs to the fifth floor chamber, where the three Jacques are peering inside through holes in the wall. Monsieur Defarge unlocks the door, and he, Mr. Lorry, and Lucie enter the room. Inside the darkened room, they see a white-haired man sitting on a bench making shoes.

Commentary

Style & Language

Dickens leaves no doubt that the crowd scene in front of the wine shop is a glimpse of things to come. The wine soaking into the street and smearing people's faces and hands represents the blood that the people will shed during the violence of the Revolution. To reinforce that imagery, Dickens goes so far as to have one of the men in the crowd dip his finger in the muddy wine and write "Blood" on a wall. As Dickens predicts future violence, he also hints at how hunger, want, and anger will transform decent, caring human beings into unthinking, bloodthirsty animals. He describes some of the wine drinkers as having "a tigerish smear about the mouth," and the residents of Saint Antoine have a "hunted air" and harbor a "wild-beast thought of the possibility of turning at bay." The image of the tiger will appear again later in the book, as will the vision of an oppressed people losing their humanity in their anger and quest for revenge.

This chapter also introduces Monsieur and Madame Defarge, characters that Dickens uses to embody the ideas and emotions of the Revolution. Monsieur Defarge is a man of authority, as shown when he reprimands Gaspard for writing "Blood" on the wall and in his conversation with the three Jacques. Although Dickens describes Monsieur Defarge as "good-humored-looking," and Monsieur Defarge demonstrates kindness and loyalty to Doctor Manette, when considering the injustice of the Doctor's imprisonment, Monsieur Defarge becomes "a secret, angry, dangerous man."

Character Insight

In the subdued atmosphere of the wine-shop, Monsieur Defarge's air of authority and resolution are exceeded only by that of his wife. Although she doesn't say much, Madame Defarge communicates secretively with her husband through coughs and facial expressions. She also seems more hardened than her husband does. While the plight of Doctor Manette enrages Monsieur Defarge, Therese Defarge remains unresponsive. When Mr. Lorry and Lucie go with Monsieur Defarge to see the Doctor, "Madame Defarge knitted with nimble fingers and steady eyebrows, and saw nothing." Her eerie calm and concentrated focus indicate a steadfastness and determination that may in the end prove more dangerous than the anger growing in the hearts of her husband and the populace of Saint Antoine.

Glossary

lee-dyed   soaked with the dregs of the wine.

Jacques   the use of the name Jacques to signify French peasants began in the peasant revolts in 1358. To maintain anonymity and to show solidarity, rebels called each other by the same name. The network of rebels using the Jacques appellation is referred to as the Jacquerie.

Notre-Dame   "Our Lady": a famous, early Gothic cathedral in Paris; the full name is Notre-Dame de Paris.

the window of dormer shape   a window set vertically in a sloping roof.

Chapter 6—The Shoemaker

Summary

The man making shoes works steadily at his bench. Aged and weakened by his long years in prison, he seems to be aware only of the task at hand—shoemaking—and does not even know that he has been released from prison. When asked his name, he responds, "One Hundred and Five, North Tower." When Lucie approaches him, however, she seems familiar to him, especially after he compares her hair to two golden hairs that he kept tied in a cloth around his neck. He begins remembering Lucie's mother and is confused and troubled when he hears Lucie's voice, which sounds like her mother's voice. Lucie embraces her father, comforting him as he begins to weep.

Later, Monsieur Defarge helps Mr. Lorry and Lucie to remove Doctor Manette from the city. As the coach carrying Mr. Lorry, Lucie, and Doctor Manette rumbles to the ship that will take them back to England, Mr. Lorry can't help looking at the man they have recovered and wondering if the Doctor will be able to be "recalled to life."

Commentary

After eighteen years of being physically and mentally removed from the world, the Doctor has suffered greatly and appears to have lost all sense of time, place, and self. Despite the fact that he is no longer in prison, he still seems "buried alive" when you first see him. Both his mind and body are hidden from view. Even after some light enters the garret where he works, the Doctor looks more dead than alive, with his hollow face, withered body, and a hand so thin that it looks transparent. Similarly, when Monsieur Defarge and Mr. Lorry try to talk to him, his mind seems starved and wasted to the point of being able to comprehend only the most basic questions and to focus solely on his work.

Literary Device

Just as light enters the garret to reveal the Doctor physically, contact with Lucie seems to awaken part of the Doctor's mind and memories. The images of light and dark that run through *A Tale of Two Cities* are especially apparent in this chapter. As Dickens literally and symbolically depicts the resurrection of the Doctor, the Doctor is drawn out of the darkness of his imprisonment and into the light of life. For instance, when for a moment the Doctor seems to nearly recognize Mr. Lorry, Dickens describes his returning blankness of expression as "a black mist" or as "darkness." Meanwhile, Lucie's face mirrors his fleeting expression of awareness "as though it had passed like a moving light from him to her." When Lucie goes to sit next to her father, his attention falls on her golden hair. He shows her his wife's golden hairs that he has kept with him and, concentrating, "turned her full to the light and looked at her." Later, when father and daughter embrace, "his cold white head mingled with her radiant hair, which warmed and lighted it as though it were the light of Freedom shining on him." The warmth and love of his daughter are strong enough to bring Doctor Manette back from the cold, colorless place his mind retreated to during his years of imprisonment.

The melodramatic sentimentality of Lucie's speeches to her father somewhat spoil the poignant reunion scene between the Doctor and Lucie. "Weep for it, weep for it!" she exclaims, and modern readers struggle not to roll their eyes or laugh aloud. However, keep in mind that the Victorians greatly enjoyed this type of melodrama, and when Lucie cried out, "Weep for it," Dickens' readers wept.

Glossary

One hundred and five, North Tower Doctor Manette's designation in the Bastille.

provender food.

pallet bed a small bed or pad filled as with straw and used directly on the floor

the box the driver's seat of a coach.

adieu French for "farewell."

Book the Second—The Golden Thread
Chapter 1—Five Years Later

Summary

Five years have passed since Tellson's Bank sent Mr. Lorry to bring Doctor Manette back to England. Tellson's continues to be "the triumphant perfection of inconvenience," with its old-fashioned dark and cramped facility lending it an air of respectability and security. Jerry Cruncher acts as a porter and messenger for the bank, and his son, who is also called Jerry, often accompanies him. At home before work one morning, the sight of his wife praying frustrates Jerry. He complains that she prays against his prosperity and tells her he won't tolerate it. After breakfast, Jerry and his son walk to Tellson's and station themselves in front of the bank before it opens. Soon the bank calls Jerry to deliver a message. Meanwhile, Young Jerry puzzles over the source of the iron rust that is always on his father's fingers.

Commentary

Dickens depicts the venerable Tellson's Bank as being in the business of death. Described as dark, ugly, and cramped, Tellson's boasts an atmosphere of deliberate grimness and decay. Money, documents, and valuables that go into Tellson's for safekeeping are buried in "wormy old wooden drawers" and acquire "a musty odor, as if they were fast decomposing" or being "corrupted."

Just as material goods are buried and decay in Tellson's, the bank transforms the people who deal with it as well. The bank hides clerks who go to work at Tellson's as young men until they become old. Additionally, Tellson's literally sends people to their deaths; the bank identifies forgers, debtors, counterfeiters, and petty thieves who eventually go to their graves under the harsh death penalty. Not coincidentally, Dickens locates Tellson's next to the Temple Bar, an arched gateway to the city where the government sometimes displayed the heads of the executed.

Jerry Cruncher, the messenger, serves as "the live sign of the house," which indicates that he may have something to do with death as well. Like many of the other characters in the novel, Jerry appears to have a secret. Some of his physical characteristics and personality traits create an air of mystery, such as his muddy boots, his rusty fingers, and his paranoia regarding his wife's prayers.

Glossary

bank note a promissory note issued by a bank, payable to the bearer on demand and which can be used as money.

plate tableware, often made of silver or covered with a layer of silver (plated).

Barmecide room a room in which things are an illusion. Barmecide was a prince in the *Arabian Nights* who offered a beggar a feast and set an empty plate before him.

purloiner a thief.

Whitefriars a dostrict of central London between Fleet Street and the Temple area where criminals and fugitive debtors lived.

personal board a person's daily meals.

choused cheated, swindled.

hackney coach a coach for hire, oftentimes a six-seat carriage drawn by two horses.

laudanum a solution of opium in alcohol or wine used as a painkiller or sleeping aid, or drunk as an intoxicant.

Chapter 2—A Sight

Summary

Jerry is told to take a note to Mr. Lorry at the Old Bailey law court and to stay there until Mr. Lorry needs him. After arriving at the Old Bailey and giving the doorkeeper the note to deliver to Mr. Lorry, Jerry makes his way into the crowded courtroom. The court is hearing a treason case, punishable by the grisly sentence of being drawn and quartered. The accused, Charles Darnay, stands quietly and calmly before the crowd until he catches sight of Lucie and Doctor Manette, who are witnesses against him. The spectators follow his eyes and are touched by Lucie's expression of fear and sympathy for Darnay.

Commentary

Dickens uses the courtroom scene to vilify the British legal system, with the Old Bailey embodying the uncompromising harshness of the law. Charles Darnay's case in particular highlights the bloody nature of criminal sentences: If found guilty, he will be drawn, half hanged, eviscerated while still alive, beheaded, and cut into pieces.

While such a sentence is gruesome in itself, more disturbing is the avid interest the courtroom spectators take in Darnay's fate. The man who describes the sentence to Jerry speaks "with a relish" and the "eager faces" of the crowd stare at Darnay with an "Ogreish" fascination. Dickens points out that such an interest in a condemned man is "not the sort that elevated humanity."

As Dickens shows repeatedly throughout the novel, crowds can bring out the basest natures of people. Interestingly, the one thing capable of elevating the sensitivities of the crowd is the sight of Lucie Manette's concern and pity for the prisoner.

Glossary

Old Bailey London's historic main criminal court on Old Bailey Street.

Tyburn public hangings in London took place at gallows called the Tyburn Tree until 1783.

pillory a device consisting of a wooden board with holes for the head and hands, in which petty offenders were formerly locked and exposed to public scorn; the stocks.

a trap a hinged or sliding door in a roof, ceiling or floor, which lifts or slides to cover an opening.

Bedlam the Hospital of St. Mary of Bethlehem, a London insane asylum, where Londoners went to watch the mentally unstable for entertainment.

Chapter 3—A Disappointment

Summary

The trial begins with the Attorney-General's long and often-times digressive statement of the treason charges against Darnay. Darnay's counsel, Mr. Stryver, attempts to discredit the prosecution's two main witnesses—John Barsad and Roger Cly—but the turning point in the trial comes when Stryver's associate, Sydney Carton, alerts him to the remarkable physical resemblance between Carton and Darnay. Stryver dramatically calls attention to the resemblance during the questioning of another witness for the prosecution, casting doubt onto the man's testimony that he saw Darnay waiting for someone in a hotel. Stryver then concludes the case with witnesses and a summation that paint Barsad as the spy and traitor and Cly as his accomplice. Darnay, he states, is an innocent victim whose confidential family affairs caused him to travel between the two countries. After an hour and a half, the jury returns with a verdict—Darnay is innocent.

Commentary

Here we see another instance of a man being "recalled to life," as Doctor Manette was in Book I. Dickens describes Darnay as being a dead man, and the crowd, which buzzes like "a cloud of great blue-flies" would over a dead body, views him as such. The dead man is saved this time, not by Mr. Lorry or Lucie, but by an unlikely source—Sydney Carton, the disinterested and disreputable-looking lawyer who spends most of his time staring at the ceiling.

Carton's apparent lack of interest in his surroundings recalls Madame Defarge's attention to her knitting; both characters appear to see nothing, yet the reader senses that they notice more than most. Carton, for example, not only discerns the striking resemblance between himself and Darnay, but also observes Lucie's faint before the other characters. Such actions suggest that Carton is a more compli-cated man than his outward appearance initially suggests.

Glossary

immolate to offer or kill as a sacrifice.

debauched corrupted by drunkenness or sensuality; depraved.

Chapter 4—Congratulatory

Summary

Doctor Manette, Lucie, Mr. Lorry, and Mr. Stryver congratulate Darnay on the verdict. After the group disperses, Carton approaches Darnay and invites him to a nearby tavern for dinner. Once there, Carton's erratic behavior bewilders Darnay. When Darnay tries to thank Carton for his assistance in the trial, Carton shrugs off the thanks and informs Darnay that he doesn't particularly like him. Despite this disclosure, Darnay reiterates his appreciation, pays the bill, and politely excuses himself. Before Darnay can leave, however, Carton confesses that he is drinking heavily because, "I am a disappointed drudge . . . I care for no man on earth, and no man on earth cares for me."

After Darnay leaves, Carton reflects that, despite their physical resemblance, the differences between them are great. Darnay embodies what Carton could have been. Carton muses that if he had been like Darnay, he might have the opportunity of being cared about by Lucie. Carton finishes his drink and falls asleep on the table.

Commentary

Character Insight

Central to the theme of doubles and mirror-images that run through *A Tale of Two Cities* are the characters of Sydney Carton and Charles Darnay. The previous chapter established their physical similarities; this chapter establishes the differences in their temperaments. Where Darnay is polite, composed, and a gentleman, Carton is ill-mannered, unkempt, and a heavy drinker. Dickens uses the contrast between the two men to emphasize the degree to which Carton is wasting his life, with Darnay serving as a representation of Carton's unrealized possibilities. Dickens stresses this point in Carton's moment of self-reflection in front of the mirror. Contemplating his hostile feelings for Darnay, Carton muses, "He shows you what you have fallen away from, and what you might have been." What Carton has fallen away from is the possibility of a happy life with someone like Lucie Manette.

Glossary

Bastille a state prison in Paris that held many prisoners indefinitely without trial; it was stormed and destroyed (1789) in the French Revolution: its destruction is commemorated on Bastille Day, July 14.

robing room the room where judges and lawyers put on their official robes.

the reckoning the bill.

winding sheet a cloth in which the body of a dead person is wrapped for burial; shroud. Also refers to solidified candle drippings, signifying death.

Chapter 5—The Jackal

Summary

After a waiter at the tavern awakens him, Carton walks from the tavern to Stryver's chambers. The two work on some cases, with Carton doing the brunt of the work. When they finish, Carton and Stryver discuss their school days together and the differences in their fortunes—how Stryver moved ahead in his profession while Carton remained in Stryver's shadow. The discussion turns to Lucie, whom Stryver admires and whom Carton dismisses as "a golden-haired doll." With dawn breaking, Carton heads home, envisioning for a moment how much richer his life might have been if he had been a man who practiced self-denial and perseverance. Facing the reality of his empty room, he goes to bed, falling asleep on a pillow wet with tears.

Commentary

Continuing the development of Carton's character, Dickens establishes Carton's failure to live up to his professional potential by comparing him with Stryver. Although the two men went through school together and have shared similar professional opportunities, Carton remains the jackal (researcher and assistant) to Stryver's lion (prominent lawyer). Carton is undoubtedly more intelligent than Stryver, but he lacks the ambition and resolve that make Stryver a success. Stryver notes that Carton seems out of sorts that evening, and indeed, the events of the trial have obviously stirred up feelings of dissatisfaction in Carton.

As he makes his way home, the setting reflects Carton's feelings of emptiness and unhappiness: "the air was cold and sad, the dull sky overcast, the river dark and dim, the whole scene like a lifeless desert." When he imagines "a mirage of honorable ambition, self-denial, and perseverance" in which love, life, and hope are all possibilities, Carton reveals his awareness of his wasted potential. His bitterness toward Darnay and his shortness with Stryver reflect the feelings of regret that have arisen in him upon seeing the one person he knows could redeem him—Lucie Manette—and knowing that his choices have put her forever out of his reach.

Glossary

Bacchanalian propensities a tendency toward drinking alcohol.

the Sessions meetings of legal officials to transact court business.

Hilary Term and Michaelmas the terms during which the courts heard cases. Hilary Term lasted from January 11-31, and Michaelmas term lasted from November 2-25.

jackal someone who performs menial tasks for another.

perspective-glass any device that aids a person's vision, like opera glasses.

Chapter 6—Hundreds of People

Summary

Four months have passed since the trial, and Mr. Lorry, Charles Darnay, and Sydney Carton have become regular visitors at the Manettes' home in Soho, where Miss Pross, Lucie's governess, also lives. While there one Sunday, Mr. Lorry and Miss Pross discuss the numerous suitors for Lucie's hand and the progress of Doctor Manette's recovery, and Darnay tells a story of a prisoner in the Tower of London who wrote the word "dig" on a wall. Years later, when workmen found the old cell, they dug into the floor beneath the inscription and found ashes of a paper inside a leather case. Doctor Manette reacts badly to this story, jumping as if startled and looking ill.

Later in the evening, as the group drinks tea and listens to the rain, they hear the echoes of people's footsteps from other streets. Lucie shares a fancy she has sometimes that the echoing footsteps are "the echoes of all the footsteps that are coming by-and-by into our lives." Carton comments that by the sound of the footsteps, there will be "a great crowd coming one day into our lives."

Commentary

Dickens refers to the Doctor's imprisonment twice in this chapter, first in the discussion between Mr. Lorry and Miss Pross and then in the Doctor's response to Darnay's story. Both incidents are reminders that the reasons behind the imprisonment are still a mystery; the Doctor is keeping secret who imprisoned him and why. The Doctor's startled response to Darnay's story indicates that he may have left a clue to his imprisonment in the cell where he was kept.

Dickens also makes clear to the reader that Lucie serves as the emotional center of the novel. Earlier in the book, he described her as a "golden thread" running through the Doctor's life and keeping him sane. Similarly, in this chapter, Dickens states that "everything turned upon her and revolved about her," suggesting that her sphere of influence extends beyond her father and encompasses all who come in contact with her. Lucie's effect on people indicates that she is the golden thread running through the entire novel. She possesses some quality that draws people to her and inspires them to be more than they are; for instance, her father has become more than a shoemaking prisoner, and Mr. Lorry has become more than a businessman. Similarly, Darnay and Carton both appear to be courting Lucie, demonstrating a desire to advance their lives from bachelorhood to marriage. As the book progresses, her influence on them will become evident in increasingly dramatic ways.

Literary Device

Making Lucie—a rather two-dimensional character—so central to the book may seem strange, but keep in mind that Dickens created Lucie to be an ideal rather than a real woman. She represents all that is good in humanity—innocence, kindness, faith, and hope—and she serves as a touchstone for other characters to find those qualities within themselves. Her premonition at the end of the chapter that she hears the echoes of the footsteps of those who will enter their lives, along with Carton's statement that crowds of people will be entering their lives, implies that these higher qualities of humanity will be challenged in the future.

Glossary

the lower regions the area of a house where servants often resided and where one could find the kitchen.

sons and daughters of Gaul that is, French men and women.

a fit of the jerks an epileptic seizure.

the Tower the Tower of London, a fortress made up of several buildings on the Thames in London, where the English government held criminals charged with high crimes.

footpad a highwayman who travels by foot.

Chapter 7—Monseigneur in Town

Summary

A reception at the Parisian suite of Monseigneur, a French lord, showcases the excesses and superficiality of the French aristocracy. The Marquis St. Evrémonde angrily leaves the reception after being snubbed by the other guests and treated coldly by Monseigneur. As his driver carouses recklessly through the Paris streets, the carriage accidentally runs over a child. The Marquis shows no remorse for the child's death, and when Gaspard, the child's grief-stricken father, approaches the carriage, the Marquis throws him a coin. Defarge emerges from the crowd to comfort Gaspard, and the Marquis throws him a coin as well. The carriage begins to move on, and one of the peasants throws a coin back into the carriage. Angered, the Marquis threatens the crowd and then drives away.

Commentary

Literary Device

Dickens uses the Monseigneur's reception to display the extravagances of the French aristocracy and to emphasize how unnatural the members of the French upper class have become. Aristocrats such as the Monseigneur have become so immersed in the spectacle of the "Fancy Ball" that they have lost touch with reality. They place themselves at the center of the world, above God and above vocation. The Monseigneur spurns the supremacy of God, for instance, when he replaces "the Lord" with "Monseigneur" in the Biblical phrase "The earth and the fullness thereof are mine, saith the Lord" and when he removes his sister from a convent in order to gain money through her marriage to a wealthy member of the Farmer-General. Other aristocrats pursue an empty life of posturing and ignorance, especially in regard to their occupations. Gentlemen had no idea how to be military or civil officers, and women of the ruling class cared nothing for motherhood.

As with other characters throughout the book, Dickens uses physical appearance to represent the moral qualities of the French nobles. "The leprosy of unreality" disfigures the people attending the reception.

Self-absorption and greed similarly disfigure their hearts and minds. The Marquis St. Evrémonde, with his attractive "face like a fine mask" that changes to look treacherous and cruel, represents all that is evil in the French aristocracy.

If the aristocracy does not care about God or about finding meaning in their lives, they certainly will give no thought to the lives of the lower classes. The incident with the Marquis and the child illustrates this disregard for the common people. By believing he can pay for a child's life like a piece of merchandise, the Marquis reveals himself to be heartless and supremely arrogant. Meanwhile, the silent challenge offered by Defarge and Madame Defarge at the scene suggests that the people's tolerance for such cruel treatment is near the breaking point.

Glossary

escutcheon the shield on which a family displays its crest.

the merry Stuart who sold it Charles II.

a Farmer-General a member of a rich organization that made a living off of high taxes.

Convulsionists members of a religious group with physical practices similar to the Shakers or the Holy Rollers.

cataleptic having a condition in which consciousness and feeling seem to be temporarily lost and the muscles become rigid: the condition may occur in epilepsy, schizophrenia, and other such conditions.

finger post a sign post.

Dervishes members of any of various Muslim religious groups dedicated to a life of poverty and chastity. Some dervishes practice whirling, chanting, and the like as religious acts.

Palace of the Tuileries where the French king and queen lived in Paris.

Chapter 8—Monseigneur in the Country

Summary

As the Marquis travels from Paris to the Evrémonde country estate, he rides through a landscape of sparse and withered crops. When his carriage stops in a village near his home, the Marquis questions a road mender who claims he saw a man riding under the carriage, but the man is no longer there. Having alerted the village official, Gabelle, to be on the lookout for the mystery man, the Marquis drives on. Before he can reach his estate, however, a grief-stricken woman stops him at the graveyard and begs him for a marker for the grave of her dead husband. Ignoring her pleas, the Marquis continues on to his chateau. When he arrives, he asks if "Monsieur Charles" has arrived from England yet.

Commentary

Literary Device

The bleak setting through which the Marquis rides testifies that the irresponsible habits of the ruling class starve the land as much as they starve the common people. Reminiscent of the spilled wine smearing the faces and hands of the people of Saint Antoine, the setting sun bathes the Marquis in a crimson light, symbolically covering him in blood. Whether the blood represents that of the dying peasants, the child he just killed, or his own bloody death is uncertain. What is certain is that, like many other members of his class, the Marquis concerns himself only with his own well-being and can't be bothered with the fate of the people who rely upon him for their lives. He is very interested, for example, in the whereabouts of the man the road mender spotted beneath his carriage but is indifferent to the plight of the widow at the graveyard.

Glossary

fagged up a steep hill toiled up the hill slowly and strenuously.

the heavy drag a brake used to slow the carriage down as it descended the hill.

a forest for the chase the wood where hunting took place.

the chain of the shoe a chain beneath the carriage, attached to the brake.

flambeau a torch.

Chapter 9—The Gorgon's Head

Summary

Once inside the chateau, in his elegant private rooms, the Marquis prepares for supper and awaits his nephew's arrival. When his nephew—Charles Darnay—arrives, the two exchange brief formalities and then, after the servants have left, Darnay tells his uncle that he is renouncing all ties to his family and to France. Although he is coolly polite, the Marquis' dislike for his nephew is apparent. Darnay equally despises his uncle, and the fear and hatred inspired by the Evrémond name troubles him. Before they part, the Marquis asks about Darnay's relationship with Doctor Manette and Lucie and then smiles mysteriously. In the morning, the Marquis is discovered dead—stabbed by a member of the Jacquerie.

Commentary

Literary
Device

With the murder of the Marquis—a man who represents evil in the aristocracy—by a representative of the common people, the tension and momentum build and the reader senses that the Revolution is near. This uprising is acted out not only in the murder, but also in Darnay's rejection of his uncle and his country. Darnay's real name, the reader discovers, is Evrémonde, meaning "everyman," and his ambition is to fulfill his mother's dying wish to right his family's wrongs. Consequently, Darnay can be viewed as the embodiment of the belief in every man's right to fairness and justice. When he renounces his family name and property, the act is as revolutionary as a peasant murdering a lord.

Glossary

the Gorgon's head in Greek mythology, a Gorgon is one of three sisters with snakes for hair. They are so horrible that a beholder is turned to stone.

a letter de cachet a document containing a royal warrant for the imprisonment without trial of a specified person.

Chapter 10—Two Promises

Summary

A year after the assassination of the Marquis, Darnay has made a life for himself in England as a tutor of French language and literature. He has been in love with Lucie since the trial, and he finally decides to speak to Doctor Manette about his feelings. Darnay tells the Doctor that he loves Lucie and wishes to marry her. Because he is unsure of Lucie's feelings for him, Darnay asks the Doctor not to say anything to her unless she discloses similar feelings for Darnay. In that case, Darnay asks the Doctor to tell her that Darnay has expressed his love for her and to not say anything against him. The Doctor agrees, but when Darnay tries to reveal his real name and background, Doctor Manette stops him and makes him promise not to divulge the information until the morning of Darnay and Lucie's wedding. That evening, Lucie finds the Doctor hammering at his shoemaker's bench. When she calls to him, he stops and makes no mention of his relapse or of Darnay's visit.

Commentary

Style & Language

The Doctor's response to Darnay's declaration of love for Lucie indicates that the Evrémonde family ties may yet have the power to disrupt his life. Additionally, Dickens has dropped hints that Darnay or his family has something to do with the Doctor's secret. The Doctor has looked at Darnay with dislike, distrust, and fear on occasion, even though Darnay has done nothing to cause offense. Similarly, the secret smile that the Marquis wore when questioning Darnay about Doctor Manette strongly suggests that he knows something about the Doctor's history.

Chapter 11—A Companion Picture

Summary

The same night that Darnay makes his declaration to Doctor Manette, Stryver tells Carton that he has decided to marry Lucie. Stryver feels that he is doing Lucie a favor by making her his wife; she is not rich, but she is "a charming creature" who will make a nice home for him. After describing how eligible and attractive he is to women, Stryver chastises Carton for making himself so unattractive to women. He recommends that Carton find himself a wife to take care of him, all the while missing the sarcasm in Carton's replies.

Commentary

Literary
Device

As the title of the chapter ("A Companion Picture") suggests, the scene between Stryver and Carton mirrors the scene between Darnay and Doctor Manette. Whereas Darnay was respectful, humble, and sincere in his discussion with the Doctor, Stryver is pompous, self-absorbed, and obnoxious. Stryver's views of marriage represent the traditional Victorian view of marriage, as something done for practical reasons. Darnay's desire to wed Lucie stems from a more idealized romantic viewpoint. He loves Lucie and only wants her to marry him if she loves him as well.

Chapter 12—The Fellow of Delicacy

Summary

Having decided to wed Lucie, Stryver heads to Soho to let her know of her good fortune. On the way, he drops by Tellson's Bank to share his marriage plans with Mr. Lorry. Rather than risk making Doctor Manette or Lucie uncomfortable by receiving a proposal directly from Stryver, Mr. Lorry suggests that Stryver let him visit the Manettes and find out if Lucie would accept Stryver's suit. Stryver agrees, and when Mr. Lorry returns from Soho, he tells Stryver that he should drop his suit. However, Stryver has already changed his mind and acts as if the incident was all a misunderstanding caused by Lucie.

Commentary

Character Insight

Stryver's sense of self-importance is so great that it physically manifests itself as he shoulders his way through the London streets and seems to fill Tellson's already-cramped space. His outraged disbelief that Lucie would be anything but thrilled by a proposal from him reinforces the worthiness of Darnay's humble courtship. Similarly, Stryver's obtuseness highlights Mr. Lorry's strengths—his diplomacy, his deep attachment to the Manettes, and his ability to take control of a stressful situation. These strengths will prove invaluable to the Manettes as the novel progresses.

Glossary

Vauxhall Gardens London's first amusement park; the gardens, located on the south bank of the Thames River, opened in 1660 and closed in 1859. Visitors enjoyed not only the natural setting, but also food, drink, musical performances, fireworks, and balloon launches.

Ranelagh a competitor of Vauxhall Gardens, open from 1742 to 1803 and famous for its masquerades.

Chapter 13—The Fellow of No Delicacy

Summary

One August afternoon, Carton resolves to reveal his feelings to Lucie. He tells her that although he is a hopeless case and can never reform, she revived his old dreams of leading a good life. Lucie suggests that he may still be able to redeem his life, but Carton states that it is too late; he knows his nature, and he will only sink lower. However, he wants her to know how deeply he loves her and that he would freely give his life for her and anyone she loved.

Commentary

Character Insight

Many characters have secrets in *A Tale of Two Cities*, but none reveals itself as painfully as Sydney Carton's does. He loves without hope, and his love for Lucie has made him aware of how much potential happiness he has squandered through his dissolute lifestyle. He tells her, "I am like one who died young. All my life might have been." Carton's situation somewhat parallels Doctor Manette's imprisonment: As a young man, Carton has buried himself alive with a long, empty life stretching before him. The strength of his love for a woman gives him the dream of freedom, but it also torments him because he cannot have her. Unlike Doctor Manette, however, Carton inflicted his own imprisonment, and he lacks the strength to recall himself to life.

Chapter 14—The Honest Tradesman

Summary

As Jerry Cruncher sits outside Tellson's Bank, he notices a funeral procession approaching. People yelling "Spies!" surround the hearse and the mourning coach, and Cruncher discovers that the funeral belongs to Roger Cly, one of the spies who testified against Darnay. When the crowd tries to pull the sole mourner out of his coach, the mourner flees the scene. The crowd then begins to pull the coffin out of the hearse, but decides to accompany it to the graveyard instead. Cruncher joins the unruly procession, which grows larger as it moves along. When the coffin is finally buried, the mob begins assaulting passersby and ransacking businesses until a rumor of the police approaching breaks up the mob. Meanwhile, Cruncher returns to Tellson's, stopping at a surgeon's on the way.

Later that night, after seeing his wife and son to bed, Cruncher leaves his house carrying a sack, a crowbar, a rope, and a chain. Curious about his father's mysterious nightly activities, Young Jerry follows Cruncher. Two men join Cruncher as he walks along, and the trio soon reaches the graveyard. As Young Jerry watches with horror, Cruncher and his companions dig up a coffin and begin to pry it open. Young Jerry rushes home, terrified that the coffin is hopping after him, and he awakes the next morning to find his father beating his mother. As Young Jerry walks to Tellson's with Cruncher, he asks his father what a "resurrection man" is. When Cruncher explains that it is a person who sells people's bodies, Young Jerry pleases his father by saying that he wants to be a resurrection man when he grows up.

Commentary

Literary Device

Dickens uses the funeral procession to demonstrate how easily a rowdy crowd can become a destructive mob. The actions of the crowd turn a solemn occasion—a funeral—into a festive one, with many of the crowd members not even aware of the cause of the uproar. The

momentum of the mob has swept them up, and they follow whatev
spontaneous commands they hear. In this way, rational, thinking ind
viduals become mindless members of a violent entity. For Dicken
mobs are unstoppable forces, frightening in their inhumanity.

Within the funeral mob, however, one man pursues his own pr
vate agenda. Jerry Cruncher, the reader discovers, is a resurrectio
man—a grave robber—and views Cly's funeral as a business opportu
nity. Cruncher's work as a resurrection man parodies the resurrectio
theme that runs through *A Tale of Two Cities*. Whereas people such a
Doctor Manette or the French peasants metaphorically return fro
their living graves through love or revolution, Cruncher literally dig
fresh corpses from their graves to sell to surgeons or medical student

Glossary

bear leader someone who lead a trained bear from place to place f
money.

public house a tavern or an inn that provided food and drink.

Izaak Walton (1593–1683); the author of *The Compleat Angler*,
fishing manual.

resurrection man a man who digs up corpses to sell to surgeons o
medical schools for study.

Chapter 15—Knitting

Summary

The mender of roads who spotted the man under the Marquis St. Evrémonde's carriage accompanies Defarge to the wine-shop. In the garret where Doctor Manette stayed, Defarge and Jacques One, Two, and Three listen to the road-mender describe what happened to Gaspard, the man who killed the Marquis. Gaspard, who murdered the Marquis for running down his child, went into hiding for nearly a year after the killing. The French authorities recently captured, jailed, and hanged him, and left his corpse dangling by the village fountain, with his shadow poisoning the atmosphere of the town.

Monsieur and Madame Defarge later take the road-mender to Versailles, where the splendor of the court dazzles him. Caught up in the emotion of the experience, the road-mender cheers the King, Queen, and other nobles. The Defarges commend his behavior, feeling that it will fuel the courtiers' arrogance and ignorance of the revolutionary movement. Additionally, the Defarges believe that the sight of such luxury and finery will supply the road-mender with a focus for his hatred and violence in the future.

Commentary

Gaspard's tortured death demonstrates how the cycle of violence in France is escalating: The Marquis killed Gaspard's child with no regret, Gaspard retaliated by killing the Marquis, and then the French government hunted down and executed Gaspard. As a result, Madame Defarge condemns the entire Evrémonde family to death in her register. From Dickens' perspective, violence can only lead to violence, and an uprising of the oppressed in France is inevitable.

As influential members of the revolutionary movement, the Defarges represent different aspects of the rebellion. Both are leaders, but Defarge focuses on organizing the Jacquerie while Madame Defarge records in her knitted registry the names of people marked for death. Defarge's actions so far reveal him to be a man who values fairness and justice. His principles, for example, caused him to risk his life

presenting a petition to the King to save Gaspard. On the other han
Madame Defarge shows little concern for anything but her register
death. The mender of roads fears her implacable demeanor, and wh
he asks her what she makes, she replies, "Shrouds." While Defar
seems to be working toward a system that will serve justice and sa
lives, Madame Defarge works single mindedly toward a system
revenge and death.

Glossary

crag a steep, rugged rock that rises above others or projects from
rock mass.

shroud a cloth used to wrap a corpse for burial; winding sheet.

Chapter 16—Still Knitting

Summary

As the road-mender departs for home and the Defarges return to Saint Antoine, a policeman who is a member of the Jacquerie informs Defarge to be alert for a new spy in the area, John Barsad. When they reach the wine-shop, the Defarges discuss the progress of the revolutionary activity. Defarge admits that the slowness of the process makes him tired and depressed, and he worries that they won't live to see their work come to fruition. Showing a rare hint of sympathy, Madame Defarge acknowledges that laying the groundwork for monumental change takes a long time. However, she adds that once the Revolution comes, it will be unstoppable, like lightning or an earthquake.

The next day, John Barsad visits the wine-shop and questions the Defarges about the unrest in Saint Antoine caused by Gaspard's execution. Both Defarges behave as if they don't know what he's talking about and, as Barsad attempts more conversation, Madame Defarge knits his name and description into her register. Barsad finally provokes an emotional response from Defarge when he mentions that Lucie Manette is engaged to marry Charles Darnay, the nephew of the Marquis St. Evrémonde. After Barsad leaves, Defarge remarks that he hopes destiny keeps Lucie and Darnay from France. Meanwhile, Madame Defarge knits Darnay's name into her register next to Barsad's.

Commentary

The differences between Defarge and his wife make themselves even more apparent after their return from Versailles. While Defarge shows a very human weariness with the seemingly endless road of revolution, Madame Defarge remains unswerving in her commitment to the cause. She views the movement as a creation process that will produce the relentless forces of vengeance and retribution. She explains to her husband, though, that "it is your weakness that you sometimes need to see your victim and your opportunity, to sustain you." In other words, the promise of an ultimate fulfillment drives Madame Defarge, while Defarge thrives on the concrete reality of day-to-day experience.

Character Insight

The private moment between the couple after their day of indoctrinating the road-mender also highlights how completely their revolutionary work has consumed them. Defarge's depression that the may not live to see the fruition of their efforts reminds the reader th the Defarges are childless, and in effect, the Revolution is their chil. Just as Doctor Manette finds new life in his daughter, Defarge hop to find a new life for himself and his country through the Revolutio However, like the aristocratic women, Madame Defarge is an unna ural mother. She works not toward giving life but toward giving deat

The Defarges' differing focuses on life and death especially emer, when Barsad discloses the news of Lucie's engagement and Darnay identity. As Defarge hopes for their sake that they stay out of Fran and therefore keep their lives, Madame Defarge coolly knits Darnay name into her register next to Barsad's, condemning them both to deat

Glossary

Christian name the baptismal name or given-name, as distinguishe from the surname or family name; first name.

catechist a person who teaches, especially the principles of a religio. by the method of questions and answers.

Chapter 17—One Night

Summary

The night before Lucie's wedding, she and her father sit outside and discuss her upcoming marriage. Lucie tells her father how happy she is and assures him that her love for Darnay will not interfere with their relationship. Doctor Manette responds by telling her that marriage is a natural step for her to take and that he is grateful that his imprisonment has not shadowed her life as it has his. He relates to her that when he was in prison he would think of the child he had never known and wonder what its fate was. No matter what he imagined, though, he could never have imagined the degree of happiness that Lucie brought into his life.

Commentary

Literary Device

Dickens juxtaposes the idyllic scene of Lucie and her father with the previous scene between the Defarges in the wine-shop. Both pairs take a quiet moment out of their busy lives to assess where their lives are going. For the Manettes, the future is bright and hopeful, filled with the promise of love and children. Lucie's happiness is a triumph for the Doctor because he has successfully kept his sorrows and hardships from tainting her future. However, the only future the Defarges look forward to is one of vengeance and retribution. The Doctor notes that "there was a time in my imprisonment, when my desire for vengeance was unbearable," but through Lucie's care he has overcome that need for revenge. The Defarges cannot separate themselves from the desire for retribution and, therefore, know none of the overwhelming happiness and hope that the Doctor feels.

Glossary

apocryphal of doubtful authorship or authenticity; not genuine.

Chapter 18—Nine Days

Summary

On the morning of Lucie and Darnay's wedding, Doctor Manett and Darnay engage in a private discussion. Afterwards, the Doctor very pale but composed. Lucie and Darnay are married and depart o a two-week honeymoon. Mr. Lorry and Miss Pross escort a subdue Doctor Manette home. Observing hints of the Doctor's former ment incapacity, Mr. Lorry tells Miss Pross that although he must take ca of some business, he will return soon. When he returns, the Doctor h regressed to his previous state of total absorption in his shoemaking an appears not to know Mr. Lorry or Miss Pross. The situation continue for nine days, and Mr. Lorry arranges that neither the Doctor's patien nor Lucie and Darnay know about the Doctor's relapse. Mr. Lorry als takes an unprecedented leave of absence from Tellson's to stay at th Manette home and watch over his friend.

Commentary

Darnay's disclosure of his name and background to Doctor Manett seems to have confirmed the Doctor's fears of his son-in-law's famil connections. Although the Doctor has been healthy physically and men tally for many years, his relapse reveals that he can still be deeply hur by his past. His vulnerability heightens the sense of foreboding sur rounding the entire family. The reader knows that the Defarges hav identified and registered Darnay; in fact, the revolutionaries have con demned the entire Evrémonde line, including any children that resul from Darnay and Lucie's marriage.

Glossary

chaise any of several kinds of lightweight carriage used for leisure having two or four wheels and drawn by one or two horses. Som have a collapsible top.

Chapter 19—An Opinion

Summary

On the tenth morning, Doctor Manette awakens fully recovered and unaware that anything unusual has transpired. Mr. Lorry tactfully conveys to the Doctor what has happened and asks what caused the relapse and how it can be prevented. The Doctor explains that he expected the relapse, which was caused by the revival of certain memories. He believes that the worst is over and doubts that another relapse could occur; if one did, it would most likely result from an intense experience that revived those same memories.

Mr. Lorry also questions the wisdom of keeping the shoemaking bench and materials, pointing out that their presence reminds the Doctor of the past that has caused him so much pain. Uneasily agreeing, Doctor Manette requests that Mr. Lorry dispose of the bench and tools without him. Therefore, Mr. Lorry and Miss Pross bury the tools and burn the shoemaking bench after the Doctor leaves to join Lucie and Darnay on their trip.

Commentary

Character Insight

One of the criticisms of *A Tale of Two Cities* is that it lacks the characters of depth and complexity that one usually associates with Dickens' novels. However, Doctor Manette is perhaps the one exception to this criticism. In his conversation with Mr. Lorry, he displays the multifaceted nature of his character, ranging from a loving father to a capable professional to a nervous victim. Although troubled by his relapse, he seems more confident in its wake, possibly because he knew Darnay's revelation might trigger a relapse and he now believes nothing else is likely to cause it to happen again. His insistence that he is not overworked and needs to work in order to balance his mind displays a self-knowledge that is especially impressive in light of the complete lack of self-awareness that he exhibited when Mr. Lorry first observed him in the Paris garret.

Interestingly, his self-assurance flags only when Mr. Lorry brings the issue of the shoemaking materials. Instantly he changes from confidence to nervous fidgeting and avoiding Mr. Lorry's gaze. As Doctor Manette explains his attachment to the bench and tools, he exposes the reality and the horror of solitary imprisonment: ". . . it relieved his pain so much, by substituting the perplexity of the fingers for the perplexity of the brain, and by substituting, as he became more practised, the ingenuity of the hands, for the ingenuity of the mental torture. . . ." In other words, the bench and tools represent a refuge into which his mind can escape when faced with the remembrance of his agony of isolation.

Glossary

sagacity the quality or an instance of being sagacious; penetrating intelligence and sound judgment; wisdom.

"guineas, shillings, and bank-notes" forms of British currency.

Chapter 20—A Plea

Summary

Soon after Lucie and Darnay return from their honeymoon, Carton visits them. He takes Darnay aside and, in an unusually sincere tone, asks for Darnay's friendship and apologizes for his rudeness after the trial. Darnay is casual about the apology, but assures Carton that he has forgotten any past offences. Carton then asks permission to visit the family occasionally, and Darnay grants it. Later that evening, after Carton leaves, Darnay comments on Carton's irresponsible nature, causing Lucie to reprimand him and ask that he show Carton more consideration in the future.

Commentary

Carton's apology to Darnay and his request to visit the family show his respect for Darnay's new place in Lucie's life and his desire to remain a peripheral part of the family's life. His sincerity and earnestness in speaking to Darnay echo the tone he took in speaking to Lucie before her marriage, indicating that he is revealing the real Carton to Darnay. However, Darnay lacks Lucie's sensitivity and compassion and fails to perceive the difference in Carton's manner. When Darnay talks about Carton as "a problem of carelessness and recklessness," Dickens adds that he is speaking of Carton "as anybody who saw him as he showed himself." While this statement may seem like a defense of Darnay's remarks, it actually comments on Darnay's inability to "see" Carton's real self, even after Carton has shown it to him. In the end, Darnay receives a glimpse of Carton's worthiness through Lucie's vision of him.

Chapter 21—Echoing Footsteps

Summary

Eight years have passed, and the year is 1789. Darnay continues to prosper, and he and Lucie have had two children—a daughter named Lucie and a son who lived several years before he died. Both children have been especially fond of Carton, who visits a few times each year. Carton continues to work for Stryver, who has married a widow with three sons. Time passes peacefully for the group in England while turmoil in France seems like "a dreadful sea rising." Problems in France begin to encroach upon the lives of those in England when Mr. Lorry appears at the Manette-Darnay home one night, tired and irritable after a long day at Tellson's. Unrest in France has caused a run on the Paris branch of Tellson's Bank.

Meanwhile, in France, the residents of Saint Antoine arm themselves with every type of weapon imaginable and begin to mass in the streets, and the Defarges lead the crowd in an attack on the Bastille. Once inside the prison, Defarge goes to Doctor Manette's old cell and searches it for something. Afterward, Defarge joins a group escorting the prison's governor to the Hotel de Ville. On the way there, the crowd attacks the governor and beats him to death, and Madame Defarge cuts off his head. In the course of the turmoil, the revolutionaries rescue seven prisoners from the Bastille and put the heads of seven guards on pikes.

Commentary

Dickens contrasts the calm of life in Soho with the turbulence in Saint Antoine. Time has passed quietly for Lucie and her family, but Mr. Lorry's agitated visit indicates that their time of tranquility is over. Mr. Lorry seems to anticipate trouble when he tells the Doctor, "the hurries and forebodings by which I have been surrounded all day long have made me nervous without reason." The "hot, wild night" reflects his restlessness, and as a literal storm takes place in England, a storm of violence rises in France.

The storming of the Bastille, which occurred on July 14, 1789, began the French Revolution, and Dickens blends history with fiction in his recreation of the event. The revolutionaries did kill and behead seven guards as well as the governor of the Bastille, De Launay. They also freed seven bewildered prisoners. For the sake of the story, though, Dickens places the Defarges at the center of the incident, with Defarge coordinating the tactical aspects of the attack and Madame Defarge leading the women in a frightening display of bloodlust.

Additionally, the violence and chaos of mobs that Dickens has hinted at previously in the novel explode here with full force. He describes the mob as "a whirlpool of boiling waters," a "raging sea," and a "howling universe of passion and contention." For Dickens, the mob is a potent force that is mindless, heartless, and inescapable.

Glossary

a run of confidence a large number of customers withdrawing their money from a bank.

musket a smoothbore, long-barreled firearm, used especially by infantry soldiers before the invention of the rifle.

pikes weapons formerly used by foot soldiers, consisting of a metal spearhead a long wooden shaft.

Chapter 22—The Sea Still Rises

Summary

A week after the fall of the Bastille, the revolutionaries learn that Foulon, a hated official who they thought was dead, is alive and has been captured. Apparently Foulon, who had said that starving people could eat grass, faked his death in order to escape the revolutionaries. Upon learning that Foulon is being held at the Hotel de Ville, Madame Defarge leads a mob to the hotel. With the help of the Defarges, The Vengeance (Madame Defarge's assistant), and Jacques Three, the mob seizes Foulon, stuffs his mouth with grass, and then hangs him from a lamp post. After he dies, they behead him and put his head on a pike. The crowd then captures Foulon's son-in-law, who has ridden into Paris under heavy guard. The mob kills him and places his head and heart on pikes. The men and women of the mob return to their homes that night, still hungry but happy and hopeful for the future.

Commentary

The violence in Paris continues as Dickens again fictionalizes historical events. Joseph-Francois Foulon was an actual person who orchestrated his own funeral and was later killed in the way Dickens describes. His mock funeral and subsequent capture conveniently tie in to the resurrection theme found throughout *A Tale of Two Cities*. In describing Foulon, Dickens is sympathetic. Foulon is an elderly "wretched old sinner" who continues "entreating and beseeching for mercy" as the crowd drags him through the streets.

The mob, however, has no mind to understand mercy. Dickens depicts the process of people being transformed by the mob, stressing the change taking place in the women, who he believes should be the moral center of society. He describes the women as "a sight to chill the boldest" as they "lashed into blind frenzy, whirled about, striking and tearing at their own friends until they dropped into a passionate swoon."

Madame Defarge is especially disturbing, for she is the one woman who seems to keep her sense of self. As she plays a game of cat and mouse with Foulon, she watches him "silently and composedly" as he begs for mercy. Her behavior here demonstrates her heartlessness and potential for cruelty, preparing us for her ruthlessness in Book III.

Chapter 23—Fire Rises

Summary

One July day, a stranger approaches the road-mender and asks for directions to the Evrémonde chateau. That night, four figures set fire to the chateau and the villagers watch it burn, making no effort to put it out despite the pleas of servants from the chateau. Excited by the destruction of the chateau, the villagers threaten Gabelle, the local tax collector, who hides on his roof while the villagers pound on his door.

Commentary

Literary
Device

The rebellion begun in Paris is spreading to the countryside. Although Dickens despises mob violence, he recognizes that the abuse of the upper classes brought the country to the point of revolution, saying "Monseigneur as a class had, somehow or other, brought things to this." Dickens also continues his depiction of the Revolution as a force of nature when he describes the four members of the Jacquerie who set fire to the chateau as "East, West, North, and South." Rather than giving them names and personas, Dickens has assigned them directions. This technique conveys a sense that the revolutionaries are the "red-hot wind" blowing in every direction to raze all vestiges of the aristocracy.

Glossary

"wore a red cap now, in place of his blue one" French revolutionaries wore red caps.

sacristan a person responsible for the ceremonial equipment in a church.

tocsin an alarm bell.

Chapter 24—Drawn to the Loadstone Rock

Summary

Three more years have passed, and the French Revolution has succeeded in removing the royalty and aristocracy from power. France is still unsettled, however, and many members of the French upper classes who have fled to England use Tellson's as an information hub. One afternoon at Tellson's, Darnay and Mr. Lorry discuss Mr. Lorry's impending trip to France, where he will manage Tellson's Paris office and try to salvage some property and papers for Tellson customers. Amidst the activity in the bank, Stryver loudly commiserates with French nobles. When a letter for the Marquis St. Evrémonde surfaces, several Frenchmen and Stryver make disparaging comments about the current Marquis St. Evrémonde, unaware that they are speaking of Darnay. Darnay offers to deliver the letter to the Marquis. When Darnay reads the letter, he is troubled to find it is from Gabelle, who has been imprisoned for acting as Darnay's steward. Feeling guilty about Gabelle's imprisonment and about leaving some matters unfinished, Darnay resolves to go to France. Idealistically, he even imagines that he might be able to calm some of the revolutionary fervor. Consequently, he writes letters explaining the situation to Lucie and Doctor Manette and then departs for France alone.

Commentary

Character Insight

Although Darnay's secret departure from England for France where revolutionaries regularly imprison and kill aristocrats may seem foolish, he is acting in accordance with his nature. Darnay embodies justice and duty, and although he is devoted to his family, his sense of responsibility forbids him to turn his back on Gabelle or on his country. Additionally, Darnay remains unaware of some of the dangers, such as Madame Defarge's register, awaiting him. Because he has renounced his property and name, he thinks of himself as a common man. He does not realize, however, that the revolutionaries in France still view him as the Marquis St. Evrémonde, an aristocrat who deserves to die.

Theme

As Darnay's fate draws near, Dickens revisits the themes of resurrection and being buried alive. For instance, Darnay leaves for France to recall Gabelle, who could be executed any time, to life. Meanwhile, by going into the turbulent climate of revolutionary France, Darnay is effectively burying himself alive.

Glossary

Sardanapalus's luxury Sardanapalus (also known as Assurbanipal) was an Assyrian king renowned for his lavish lifestyle.

Prison of the Abbaye a prison in Paris that held many aristocrats during the French Revolution.

the **Loadstone Rock** a rock containing loadstone (or lodestone), a naturally magnetic mineral.

Book the Third—The Track of a Storm
Chapter 1—In Secret

Summary

Charles Darnay travels through France to Paris, encountering bands of revolutionaries in every village along the way who condemn him as an aristocrat and emigrant and allow him to continue on only because of his letter from Gabelle. A decree has passed, he learns, that sells all the property of emigrants and condemns them to death. Eventually he is forced to take an escort of two men with him. Once he arrives in Paris, a prison tribunal declares him a prisoner "in secret" of La Force prison. Defarge escorts Darnay to the prison and Darnay asks him to notify Mr. Lorry of his imprisonment. Defarge refuses. When Darnay enters the prison, the other prisoners all seem like ghosts to him. The other prisoners express their pity that he is "in secret" (Darnay doesn't know what this means). Darnay is taken to a small cell where he is locked up alone. He cannot help being reminded of Doctor Manette and thinking of Lucie.

Commentary

One thing on which the critics agree is that *A Tale of Two Cities* is masterfully plotted and structured. Dickens' genius becomes more and more apparent in the novel's third book, as the various story lines merge and the characters' lives intersect. Dickens gives the novel a circular feel as Darnay's journey and imprisonment seem to repeat events that have taken place before. His journey, for instance, parallels Mr. Lorry's trip to France in Book I. In both cases, each man travels secretly from England to release an innocent man from prison. However, where Defarge assisted Mr. Lorry, he imprisons Darnay.

Like Doctor Manette, Darnay has been locked away "in secret," with no chance of contacting family or friends and no hope of a trial. Additionally, as Darnay enters the prison and momentarily mingles with the other prisoners, he seems to be buried alive, as the Doctor once was. To him, the other prisoners appear as ghosts "all turning on him eyes that were changed by the death they had died in coming there." When he is taken to his cell, confined alone, he thinks, "Now I am left, as if I were dead." Darnay is now like a dead man, whose only hope is to be recalled to life somehow.

Glossary

dragoon trot the pace of a mounted military unit.

eventide evening.

farrier a person who shoes horses.

ambuscade ambush.

La Force a prison in Paris.

wicket a grated window in a door.

Chapter 2—The Grindstone

Summary

Mr. Lorry is troubled by the violence in the city as he sits in his rooms at the Paris branch of Tellson's Bank. Suddenly, Lucie and Doctor Manette rush into the room, and Lucie frantically tells him that the revolutionaries have taken Charles prisoner. A mob enters the courtyard outside and begins sharpening its weapons on a large grindstone there. Encouraging Lucie to be calm, Mr. Lorry sends her into another room and informs Doctor Manette that the mob is butchering the prisoners of La Force. As a former inmate of the Bastille, Doctor Manette has some influence with the revolutionaries, so he leaves to try to save Darnay's life.

Commentary

Style & Language

Dickens again dramatizes the horrors of mob violence, but this time with a twist: Doctor Manette is able influence the mob to do some good. Describing the scene at the grindstone as a vision of hell, Dickens depicts the mob members as savages and demons who work in a "wicked atmosphere" of "gore and fire." Their bloody, sweaty faces are "horrible and cruel," and the red of blood and fire is reflected "in their frenzied eyes." The sight terrifies Mr. Lorry, but Doctor Manette, whom the reader has seen when lost and demented, simply smiles "a cool bold smile" and goes down to the crowd. With his white hair and calm demeanor, the Doctor is god-like in his ability to walk through the mob unharmed, "put[ting] the weapons aside like water." His years as a prisoner have become a source of strength rather than weakness. As a former prisoner, he is a hero, and as a hero, he can rescue his daughter's husband from a living death, just as she rescued him.

Glossary

the Gazette an English government publication that listed bankruptcy announcements.

Chapter 3—The Shadow

Summary

Despite his personal devotion to Lucie and her daughter, Mr. Lorry recognizes as a businessman that keeping the family of a La Force prisoner at Tellson's could endanger the bank. Consequently, he finds a nearby apartment for them and leaves Jerry Cruncher there to protect them. The day drags on with no word from Doctor Manette. Finally that evening, Monsieur Defarge delivers a message to Mr. Lorry from the Doctor, which states that Darnay is safe for the moment and that Defarge has a note from Darnay to Lucie. As Mr. Lorry takes Defarge to see Lucie, Madame Defarge and The Vengeance join them. Defarge explains that the women want to see Lucie and her child so that they can identify and protect her, should the need arise. After reading the message from her husband, Lucie thanks Madame Defarge and begs her to help Darnay. Madame Defarge responds coldly to Lucie's entreaties. When Miss Pross and young Lucie present themselves to Madame Defarge, she barely notices Miss Pross, focusing instead on young Lucie and casting a literal and figurative shadow on both Lucie and her daughter.

Commentary

Although the news from Doctor Manette is hopeful, the menacing presence of Madame Defarge offsets it. Defarge's discomfort with the interview is apparent in his reserved manner and especially when Madame Defarge catches him worriedly biting his fingernail. Madame Defarge, on the other hand, is as cold and pitiless as ever, and the reader gets the feeling that the names and descriptions of Lucie and her daughter will shortly appear knitted into the register.

Character Insight

Madame Defarge's cold confidence causes her to make an error in judgment, however. She underestimates Lucie. Throughout the book, Dickens has shown Lucie and Madame Defarge to be opposites: Lucie represents love and compassion, while Madame Defarge represents revenge and retribution. For Dickens, Lucie encompasses all that is ideal in a woman—her morality, her kind heart, her domesticity, and her success as a wife and mother. On the other hand, Madame Defarge exemplifies the ultimate "unnatural" woman, foregoing all of the ideal qualities Lucie exhibits in order to devote her life to hatred and vengeance. What Madame Defarge cannot predict or understand is the degree of loyalty and power that Lucie commands through her loving and generous heart.

Chapter 4—Calm in Storm

Summary

After four days, Doctor Manette finally returns from the prison. He tells Mr. Lorry how he tried to influence the court tribunal to free his son-in-law, but only secured a guarantee of Darnay's safety. He also recounts the erratic behavior of the mob, which one minute would violently attack condemned prisoners and the next minute would exuberantly cheer the freeing of other prisoners. Feeling strong in his power as a Bastille survivor, Doctor Manette is confident that he will be able to free Darnay. Despite the Doctor's efforts, though, Darnay remains in prison for a year and three months. In the meantime, the Doctor becomes well known throughout Paris and gains status as the inspecting physician for three prisons.

Commentary

Darnay has been imprisoned at one of the most dangerous times in the Revolution for political prisoners. In September 1792, revolutionaries killed between 1,110 and 1,400 prisoners, about half of Paris' prison population at that time. Without Doctor Manette's influence, Darnay's captors almost surely would have killed him. The year that passes takes France into the Reign of Terror and places the Manette and Darnay family in the heart of the most violent period of the Revolution.

Literary Device

Dickens deliberately chose the timing of the story to correspond with the September Massacres and the Reign of Terror. By doing so, he is preparing a face-off between the forces of love and the forces of hate. He positions the Doctor, Darnay, and Lucie, who are bound by faith and love, against mobs motivated by violence and vengeance. His technique may seem dramatic, but it is good storytelling—it builds suspense and allows his characters to evolve and shine in ways they never could have if they had remained in their quiet Soho home.

Dickens' allusion to the dechristianization movement that was occurring at this time is also significant. In an attack on the Catholic religion, the new government stated that the only religion of France was the religion of liberty and equality. As a result, the French vandalized churches, forced priests to marry, and renamed the Notre-Dame cathedral as the "Temple of Reason." Dickens refers to the dechristianization trend when he mentions the "Year One of Liberty" and the people's worship of the guillotine instead of the cross. He sees the devil in such changes, stating that "the deluge of the Year One of Liberty" was "rising from below, not falling from above," and referring to the guillotine as "a toy-puzzle for a young Devil."

Style & Language

By naming the executioner Samson, a name from the Old Testament, Dickens indicates that the people of France are living by the vengeful law of the Old Testament—an eye for an eye, and a tooth for a tooth. They have turned away from the cross, the symbol of the New Testament, which teaches the Golden Rule—love thy neighbor. Additionally, in replacing the cross with the guillotine, the revolutionaries have transferred their faith from resurrection and redemption to retribution and death.

Glossary

Year One of Liberty the new government of France created a new calendar, based on the inception of the French Republic in 1792 rather than on the birth of Christ. Consequently, 1792 was Year One.

the head of the king. . .the head of his fair wife Louis XVI was executed on January 21, 1793. His wife, Marie Antoinette, was executed on October 18, 1793.

Chapter 5—The Wood-Sawyer

Summary

Throughout Darnay's imprisonment, Lucie goes to the prison for two hours each day hoping that her husband will be able to see her. The spot where he might view her, however, is next to a woodcutter's house. The woodcutter, formerly the road-mender, torments Lucie by pretending to saw off her and her daughter's heads; Lucie gives him money to leave her alone. One day, a wild mob comes dancing down the street and surrounds a frightened Lucie. As it moves on, Doctor Manette tells Lucie to blow Darnay a kiss because Darnay is watching. As she does so, Madame Defarge walks by and greets them. The Doctor tells Lucie that Darnay's trial is scheduled for the next day.

Commentary

Character Insight

Lucie's love and compassion distinguish her from the other characters, but she also exhibits remarkable courage in the face of frightening circumstances. Her love for Darnay prompts her to stand on an isolated street every day, regardless of weather and despite the anxiety the woodcutter must cause her. She deals with his crude nature intelligently; rather than avoiding him, she speaks to him and gives him money. Similarly, her response to the crowd whirling around her is not to shriek or swoon, but to shade her eyes and explain that such displays of madness make her fear for her husband's safety. By giving Lucie exceptional courage and selflessness, Dickens creates a character who is admirable enough to justify the devotion she inspires in others. The reader's belief that Lucie is worthy of deep attachment and sacrifice is vital to the plausibility of the plot.

Glossary

the Carmagnole a dance popular during the French Revolution.

the Conciergerie a prison in the Palais de Justice where many prisoners sentenced to die by the guillotine spent their last days.

Chapter 6—Triumph

Summary

At the trial the next day, Darnay offers an articulate and well-planned defense of himself. However, the jury remains unconvinced of his innocence until Doctor Manette and Mr. Lorry testify on his behalf. The court spectators who called for Darnay's head at the beginning of the trial cheer wildly when the jury votes to free him. As the crowd swarms around Darnay and carries him home, the rapid change in his situation bewilders him. When he reaches home, he embraces Lucie and his daughter, and he and Lucie pray together in thanks. Afterward, Lucie embraces her father, who is proud of what he has accomplished.

Commentary

The image of Lucie's head on her father's breast brings the reader full circle in the story of the father and daughter. Just as she dug him out of his mental prison, he has unearthed her husband from his prison. Darnay has been "resurrected," just as the Doctor was. However, the family's happiness must be fleeting; regardless of the innocent verdict, Madame Defarge has indelibly recorded Darnay's name in her register. Dickens shows the reader Madame Defarge, sitting in the front row "with a spare piece of knitting under her arm as she worked." That spare piece of knitting is undoubtedly the portion of the register that contains Darnay's name. Although the jury has declared Darnay innocent, one day's verdict does not mean he is safe. Dickens repeatedly has emphasized the changeable nature of the populace, even at Darnay's trial. Just as the tide of opinion shifted from bloodlust to intense support, a word from Madame Defarge can swing the tide back again.

Chapter 7—A Knock at the Door

Summary

Although the Doctor voices confidence in the validity of Darnay's release, Lucie remains fearful for her husband's safety. As the family enjoys a quiet evening together, Miss Pross leaves on a shopping expedition with Jerry Cruncher. Soon afterward, four rough men pound on the door and enter the apartment. They inform Darnay that he is a prisoner again, based on accusations from three people: Monsieur and Madame Defarge and someone else whom they refuse to name. Darnay's new trial will take place the next day.

Commentary

Darnay's re-arrest realizes Lucie's fears. Although the rough men name both Defarges as accusers, the reader knows that Madame Defarge must be the person primarily responsible. One may wonder why Madame Defarge allowed Darnay to be freed only to have him arrested again that same day. Dickens foreshadowed this move at the killing of Foulon, when Madame Defarge stayed close to Foulon in the mob and let him go before snatching him back again, like a cat with a mouse. Similarly, she allowed Darnay to experience a moment of freedom before sending him back to almost certain death. This behavior is the hallmark of cruelty, for it tortures the victim with a glimpse of what he wants the most, making him realize how much he is losing. Madame Defarge's action reveals the depths of her ruthlessness.

Glossary

dumb lacking the power of speech; speechless.

Chapter 8—A Hand at Cards

Summary

As Miss Pross and Jerry Cruncher enter a wine-shop, Miss Pross screams at the sight of a man about to leave whom she recognizes as her brother, Solomon Pross. Nervous about the attention Miss Pross is drawing to him, Solomon tells her to be quiet, and they leave the shop. Cruncher follows, trying to remember where he's seen the man before. When they reach a dark street corner, Sydney Carton, who has recently arrived in Paris, joins them and identifies Solomon Pross as John Barsad, the police spy from Darnay's trial in England. Carton states that Barsad is now a prison informer and threatens Barsad into going to Tellson's with him. Jerry accompanies the two men after they take a distraught Miss Pross to her home.

At Tellson's, Carton informs Mr. Lorry that Darnay has been arrested again and that Doctor Manette was helpless to prevent it. Carton then proceeds to intimidate Barsad, threatening to denounce him to the French authorities as an English spy. The knowledge that Roger Cly, the other police spy from England, is now in France and working as an informer strengthens Carton's case against Barsad. When Barsad protests that Cly is dead, Jerry surprises everyone by insisting that Cly's coffin contained stones and dirt. Barsad gives in and asks Carton what he wants. Carton inquires whether Barsad has access to the prison, and when Barsad says he does, Carton takes him to another room for a private conversation.

Commentary

Literary Device

A coherent picture begins to emerge from all the seemingly unrelated details of the novel. This cohesion is what makes the plot of *A Tale of Two Cities* so masterful and sets it apart from Dickens' other novels. In his other books, Dickens would include the spies Barsad and Cly, references to Miss Pross' degenerate brother, and Jerry's alternate occupation, but they wouldn't necessarily progress the main story. However, as will soon be seen, Carton's power over Barsad is essential to the conclusion of the book, and the conversion of all of these minor plot points contributes to the success of the whole.

Glossary

cavalier a gallant or courteous gentleman; originally, a knight.

spencer a short jacket that ends at the waist.

a cant word a term from the secret slang of beggars, thieves, and the like.

tergiversation the use of evasions or subterfuge.

Chapter 9—The Game Made

Summary

With Carton and Barsad in the other room, Mr. Lorry expresses his outrage at Jerry's grave robbing activities and tells Jerry that he will be fired from Tellson's. Never quite admitting his wrongdoing, Jerry asks Mr. Lorry to let his son take his place at Tellson's and tells him that he will become a regular gravedigger to make up for the bodies he dug up.

Carton and Barsad emerge from the other room, and Barsad and Jerry leave. Carton tells Mr. Lorry that the best he can do is to secure access to Darnay in his cell. Mr. Lorry begins to weep as the implications of Darnay's second arrest sink in. Moved by Mr. Lorry's tears, Carton tells him in a sincere tone that he regards him as a father-figure who has led a good and useful life, and that people will mourn Mr. Lorry and remember him when he dies. Carton adds that a long life wasted would be a miserable one. When Mr. Lorry leaves Tellson's to comfort Lucie and her father, Carton walks the streets all night with the biblical passage, "I am the resurrection and the life," echoing in his mind. At one point, he drops in at a chemist's shop to make a purchase.

The next day, Carton attends Darnay's new trial. The bloodthirsty jury includes the malevolent Jacques Three. The public prosecutor opens the trial by stating that Darnay's three accusers are the Defarges and Doctor Manette. The Doctor protests this statement, but is reprimanded. Defarge then explains that he retrieved a written paper from the Doctor's old cell in the Bastille. The paper was written by Doctor Manette and contains his denouncement.

Commentary

As the story reaches its climax, the main themes of the novel reassert themselves forcefully. Carton seems to have made some decision regarding himself and Darnay, but Dickens keeps the decision hidden, reminiscent of his earlier discussion of people's secret selves. Additionally, the resurrection theme that has recurred throughout the novel becomes unmistakable here as Carton roams the streets hearing "I am the resurrection and the life" repeatedly in his mind and in the echoes of his footsteps. Dickens also represents the resurrection theme through the transformation of a night into dawn. As the moon sets, he states, "Then, the night, with the moon and the stars, turned pale and died, and for a little while it seemed as if Creation were delivered over to Death's dominion." But then the sun rises gloriously, and as Carton looks at the sun's rays, "a bridge of light appeared to span the air between him and the sun." Dickens seems to be indicating that Carton has prepared himself to die.

The beginning of the trial reminds us that the Doctor's past remains buried. Defarge, it seems, has dug it up in the paper he found in Doctor Manette's cell, and the mysterious connection between the Doctor and Darnay is about to be revealed.

Glossary

cogitation serious, deep thought; meditation.

prevaricate to lie or to avoid telling the whole truth.

Chapter 10—The Substance of the Shadow

Summary

In December 1757, two noblemen sought out Doctor Manette and requested his medical expertise. Secretly taking him to a country house outside of Paris, the men—who Doctor Manette observed were twin brothers—ordered the Doctor to care for a delirious young peasant woman and her dying brother. The woman's brother told the Doctor that the noblemen had raped the woman and caused the deaths of the woman's husband and father. After taking a second, younger sister to safety, the young man came after the noblemen who held his sister captive. One of the brothers stabbed him, mortally wounding him. As the peasant man died, he cursed the brothers and their family line, signaling the curse with a cross of blood. The peasant woman died shortly afterward, and the brothers instructed Doctor Manette to remain silent about the incident.

Troubled by what he had witnessed, the Doctor decided to write a letter reporting the episode to the Court. Before he delivered the letter, however, the older twin's wife visited him, revealing that the brothers' family name was Evrémonde. The woman explained that she hoped the Doctor could help her to find the surviving member of the peasant family—the younger sister whom the young man had taken away. When the Doctor was unable to help her, she told her young son, Charles, to pledge himself to righting the wrong committed by his uncle and father.

Doctor Manette then personally delivered the letter and that night was kidnapped and secretly jailed by the Evrémonde brothers, who had seen his letter. At the end of his narrative, the Doctor denounced the Evrémonde family. After the document has been read, the courtroom erupts into bloodthirsty cries against Darnay, and the jury sentences Darnay to death on the following day.

Commentary

The revelation of the Doctor's secret is the climax of *A Tale of Two Cities*: The main plot of the book has led up to the discovery of who imprisoned him and why, and the disclosure of that information results in Darnay's death sentence and the subsequent events that will conclude the story.

Literary Device

Doctor Manette's narrative contains images and themes that have recurred throughout the novel. Most obvious is the image of doubleness, shown in the form of the twin Evrémonde brothers. Both men are evil, and each brother's ruthlessness seems to strengthen the other's. Through the vicious Evrémondes, Dickens makes a statement regarding the nature of violence and cruelty. Just as evil reflects evil in the two brothers, their murderous treatment of the peasant family eventually reflects back upon Darnay, the Evrémonde heir, as the French citizens demand his death. Darnay's mother recognizes the likelihood of Darnay becoming a victim of his father's sins when she tells the Doctor, "If no other innocent atonement is made for this, it will one day be required of him." Thirty-six years later, the death sentence has realized her premonition.

Glossary

quay a landing place along the bank of a river.

surgeon someone who cared for external injuries such as broken bones or wounds. Surgeons were not physicians and were referred to as "Mr." rather than "Dr."

anathematize to denounce or curse.

Chapter 11—Dusk

Summary

Darnay's death sentence devastates Lucie, but she manages to control her shock for her husband's sake. As the crowd jubilantly leaves, the court grants her permission to embrace her husband one last time. She and Darnay say their farewells, and Doctor Manette approaches them. Darnay tries to comfort his father-in-law, but the Doctor only wrings his hands and cries out. When the guards lead Darnay away, Lucie faints. Carton picks her up and carries her to the waiting coach.

Back at Lucie and the Doctor's lodgings, young Lucie begs Carton to help her parents. Carton kisses the still-unconscious Lucie goodbye, whispering, "A life you love," and then urges Doctor Manette to try to influence the judges one last time. After arranging to meet with Mr. Lorry and the Doctor later that evening, Carton leaves.

Commentary

Style & Language

As in the reunion scene between Lucie and her father in Book I, Victorian melodrama somewhat mars the poignancy of the farewell scene between Lucie and Darnay for modern readers. Dickens loads the couple's dialogue with saccharine endearments and pious sentiment. Darnay, for instance, names Lucie the "dear darling of [his] soul," while Lucie declares she will surely die from a broken heart and will join him in heaven. Perhaps the most melodramatic moment comes from Doctor Manette, who pulls his hair, wrings his hands, and shrieks in anguish. He is obviously very close to reverting back to his shoemaking state.

However, in the midst of the shrieking, fainting, and general despair, Carton displays a remarkable calmness and sense of purpose. The crisis that is devastating the lives of his friends seems to be giving him the ambition and resolve that he has always lacked. He takes control of the situation, giving the Doctor something constructive to do and comforting Mr. Lorry. When he picks up the unconscious Lucie, he has "an air about him that was not all of pity—that had a flush of pride in it."

His whispered words to Lucie, "A life you love," recall his words to he
years before when he told her "there is a man who would give his li
to keep a life you love beside you." Keeping that statement in min
the reader must conclude that when he tells Mr. Lorry, "He will perisl
there is no real hope," he is speaking of himself rather than Darnay.

Glossary

the dock the place where the accused stands or sits in court.

Chapter 12—Darkness

Summary

Deciding to make himself known to the local citizens, Carton goes to the Defarge wine-shop. Madame Defarge notices the resemblance between Carton and Darnay, but she is soon convinced that Carton is not Darnay because Carton pretends that he knows very little French. As Carton appears to be absorbed in a newspaper, the Defarges, The Vengeance, and Jacques Three discuss whether or not they should also denounce Lucie, her daughter, and Doctor Manette. Madame Defarge reveals that she is the younger sister of the peasant woman who was raped by the Evrémondes and demands vengeance for the murder of her entire family. Defarge, however, believes the killing should be limited.

After listening to the discussion, Carton goes to Mr. Lorry to tell him of the danger to Lucie and her family. The Doctor appears, reduced again to his demented state and searching for his shoemaking bench. After calming the distraught man, Carton instructs Mr. Lorry to have a carriage and everyone's passport ready at two o'clock the following afternoon.

Commentary

Dickens' plot becomes even more cohesive with the discovery of Madame Defarge's connection to the Evrémonde family. With her disclosure, she reveals the last major secret of the book, and the reason for her ruthless hatred of Darnay and all aristocrats becomes clear.

Character Insight

Madame Defarge has stood apart from the other revolutionaries in her attitude and purpose. For instance, rather than being swept up in the revolutionary fervor of a mob, she incites and controls it for her own objectives, as in the case of Foulon's death. Similarly, rather than viewing the Revolution as an agent of positive change, as her husband does, Madame Defarge regards it as an instrument of vengeance and retribution. Readers now understand that her cold-blooded rage is the product of a devastating childhood trauma. In killing her family, the Evrémonde brothers killed her heart. They also, in effect, killed their own future, for

Madame Defarge seems intent upon wiping out the entire Evrémonde line, including Darnay's innocent wife and daughter.

Literary Device

Dickens uses the relationship between the Evrémonde brothers and Madame Defarge to represent the relationship between the French aristocracy and the lower classes. As he states repeatedly throughout the book, the horrors of the French Revolution grew out of the horrors of the old regime, just as Madame Defarge's viciousness stems from the ruthlessness of Darnay's father and uncle.

Glossary

Jacobin journal the newspaper of a society of radical democrats in France during the French Revolution: so called because their meetings were held in the Jacobin friars' convent.

inveteracy persistence or tenaciousness.

Chapter 13—Fifty-two

Summary

On the eve of his execution, Darnay comes to terms with his imminent death. After writing letters to Lucie, Doctor Manette, and Mr. Lorry, he spends the night restlessly trying to sleep. The next day, Carton enters the cell at one o'clock in the afternoon and exchanges clothes with him. Then, while Carton dictates a letter to Darnay, Carton drugs him so that he loses consciousness. Two guards, who believe that Darnay is Carton and that Carton is Darnay, then carry Darnay out of the prison. At two o'clock, guards take Carton from the cell to a larger room in which the fifty-two prisoners that the court has scheduled for execution are assembling. No one notices that he is not Darnay, except for a meek little seamstress who asks Carton to hold her hand on the way to the guillotine.

Meanwhile, the coach containing Mr. Lorry, Doctor Manette, Lucie, Darnay, and young Lucie passes through the gates of Paris, where they identify Darnay—who is still unconscious—as Carton. Despite delays and fears of discovery, the group escapes France.

Commentary

Theme

The theme of doubles again appears when Carton uses his and Darnay's remarkable resemblance to save Darnay's life for a second time. The first time Carton saved Darnay, Carton did so without risk to himself. Afterward, the similarity in their features disturbed Carton, for the resemblance reminded him of the difference in their personalities and possibilities. Darnay represented everything that Carton could have been if he had not succumbed to alcohol and apathy. Saving Darnay this time, however, requires that Carton sacrifice his own life. On the surface Carton appears to make the sacrifice simply out of love for Lucie and her child. However, by considering the theme of resurrection that Dickens has woven through the story, we realize that Carton is also giving his life to save his soul. His remembrance of the "I am the resurrection and the life" passage two nights earlier indicates that he expects to find eternal life through his death. Additionally, by saving Darnay, he resurrects his best qualities in two ways. He has resurrected them in himself by planning and managing the crisis when the others could do nothing to help, and, by giving new life to Darnay, he has resurrected his own discarded potential through the man who embodies the realization of that potential.

Glossary

two score and twelve fifty-two (a score is twenty).

cravat a neckerchief or scarf.

a litter a stretcher for carrying the sick or wounded.

Chapter 14—The Knitting Done

Summary

Madame Defarge tells The Vengeance and Jacques Three that she plans to denounce Lucie, Lucie's daughter, and Doctor Manette that evening after Darnay's execution. She then leaves for Lucie's residence, knowing she will find Lucie grieving for Darnay. Showing grief for an enemy of the Republic is considered treasonous, and Madame Defarge plans to use Lucie's grief against her.

Meanwhile, Miss Pross and Jerry make preparations to leave and plan to meet up with Mr. Lorry's coach later. Anxious for the others' safety, Jerry vows that he will stop grave robbing and beating his wife for praying if Mr. Lorry and his group return safely to England. Deciding that two vehicles leaving their residence in one day might be suspicious, Miss Pross tells Jerry to wait for her with a carriage outside Notre-Dame cathedral at three o'clock.

Madame Defarge enters the apartment as Miss Pross is preparing to leave. Thinking quickly, Miss Pross closes the doors to all of the rooms and pretends to be guarding Lucie and her family. Although the two women can't understand each other's languages, they recognize that they are enemies. After calling for Lucie and the Doctor, Madame Defarge suspects that they have fled and tries to enter the room that Miss Pross is blocking. The two women struggle and Madame Defarge pulls out a gun. Miss Pross strikes it aside and the gun goes off, killing Madame Defarge and permanently deafening Miss Pross. After locking the apartment, Miss Pross rushes to the cathedral to meet Jerry and escape.

Commentary

Character Insight

Although killing off a central character like Madame Defarge in a struggle with a minor character like Miss Pross may seem odd, Dickens prepares the reader for Miss Pross' role as protector early in the novel. In our first encounter with Miss Pross, when the news that her father is alive shocks Lucie, Mr. Lorry observes Miss Pross to be the "wild-looking woman" with "a brawny hand" that sent him flying into a wall (see Book I, Chapter 2). Her response to Lucie's being even mildly threatened establishes her ability and willingness to defend "her darling." Miss Pross' single-minded devotion to Lucie and her family mirrors Madame Defarge's unwavering determination to kill Darnay, Lucie, and their family. Both women have dedicated their lives to the family, but with different purposes: Miss Pross lives to help the family flourish, while Madame Defarge lives to see them dead.

Literary Device

The final conflict between Miss Pross and Madame Defarge also represents a larger conflict between love and hate. By having Miss Pross triumph over Madame Defarge, Dickens indicates that love can conquer even the strongest hatred. Carton similarly defeats Madame Defarge when he orchestrates Darnay's freedom out of love for Lucie. However, in both cases, the struggle exacts a price for evil's defeat— Miss Pross loses her hearing and Carton loses his life. Dickens seems to be saying that good will overcome evil, but not without suffering and sacrifice.

Chapter 15—The Footsteps Die Out Forever

Summary

As the carts carrying the fifty-two prisoners roll through the Paris streets, people crowd to see Evrémonde go to his death. In his cart, Carton ignores the yelling crowds, focusing instead on the seamstress. When they reach the guillotine, they discuss the afterlife, taking no notice of prisoners steadily being executed ahead of them. They exchange a kiss before she ascends the guillotine, and he then follows her in a tranquil mood, remembering the resurrection passage from the Bible. Meanwhile, The Vengeance wonders why Madame Defarge is not there to witness Evrémonde's execution.

Before he dies, Carton has a vision of the future in which many of the revolutionaries go to the guillotine and the evil of the Revolution gives way to goodness and true freedom. In his vision, he foresees long and happy lives for Mr. Lorry, Doctor Manette, and the Darnay family, all of whom remember him lovingly. He also pictures Lucie and Darnay having a son, whom they name after him and who will become the man Carton always wanted to be. With this vision in mind, Carton goes to his death thinking, "It is a far, far better thing that I do, than I have ever done; it is a far, far better rest that I go to than I have ever known."

Commentary

Dickens concludes his book with the reiteration of several important themes. First, he emphasizes that the French Revolution is the natural result of years of oppression and extravagance on the part of the aristocracy. The carts carrying the fifty-two prisoners to their deaths parallel "the carriages of absolute monarchs, the equipages of feudal nobles." Additionally, Dickens describes the wheels of the carts as "ploughing up a long crooked furrow among the populace in the streets." This imagery recalls the personification of Death as a farmer in the first chapter of the book. In *A Tale of Two Cities*, however, death often leads to resurrection, and Dickens uses this theme to conclude the book in a tone of hope. Carton's final vision indicates that the evil inherent in the previous regime and the current Revolution will eventually wear itself out and Paris and the people of France will be resurrected, "rising from this abyss." For those dying in the Revolution, Carton assures the seamstress that they will find everlasting life "in the better land" of heaven and will reunite with their loved ones there. Finally, Carton himself finds both resurrection and redemption through his death. He not only has the comfort of being reborn into the afterlife, but is also uplifted at the thought of being resurrected, in a sense, through his namesake. In dying, Carton restores meaning to his life and the lives of those he loves.

Glossary

the seers people with the supposed power to foretell events or a person's destiny; prophets.

expiation a making amends or reparation for guilt or a wrongdoing.

CHARACTER ANALYSES

The following character analyses delve into the physical, emotional, and psychological traits of the literary work's major characters so that you might better understand what motivates these characters. The writer of this study guide provides this scholarship as an educational tool by which you may compare your own interpretations of the characters. Before reading the character analyses that follow, consider first writing your own short essays on the characters as an exercise by which you can test your understanding of the original literary work. Then, compare your essays to those that follow, noting discrepancies between the two. If your essays appear lacking, that might indicate that you need to re-read the original literary work or re-familiarize yourself with the major characters.

Doctor Alexandre Manette 96

Lucie Manette, later Darnay 96

Charles Darnay 97

Sydney Carton 97

Therese Defarge 98

Ernest Defarge 98

Jerry Cruncher 99

Doctor Alexandre Manette

A Tale of Two Cities is, in many ways, Doctor Manette's story. The Doctor's release from the Bastille begins the novel, and the mystery of his imprisonment creates tension throughout the book. The reading of his letter ultimately condemns Darnay to death, forcing Carton to sacrifice his life. Despite the Doctor's centrality to the book, however, many people portray him as a weak, pitiful character, especially in theater or film productions of *A Tale of Two Cities*. Such a perception does the Doctor and the story a great disservice.

A close reading of the book reveals the Doctor to be one of its few complex characters. Throughout the course of the novel, he is seen as an aspiring young doctor, a prisoner who craves revenge and who descends into madness, and a man who fights to regain his mind, his family, and his profession. His life after prison is a continual struggle against the shadows of madness and despair that are his legacy from the Bastille. The love he has for his daughter helps him to overcome the darkness in his life, even giving him the strength to welcome the son of his enemy as a son-in-law. When his status as a Bastille prisoner becomes an asset at the end of the book, he regains the strength and confidence that characterized him before his imprisonment. When his bitter, angry letter surfaces, however, the past undermines his stability.

Through the Doctor, Dickens makes a statement regarding the nature of forgiveness and revenge. The Doctor's ability to forgive brings him happiness in his daughter's marriage and children. However, his past demand for revenge has the power to destroy his life and the lives of his family. Additionally, whereas revenge leads the Doctor to a state of dementia, forgiveness raises him to a level of intellectual vigor and emotional happiness. In showing these contrasting aspects of Doctor Manette's character, Dickens emphasizes the concepts of the destructive power of revenge and the healing power of forgiveness.

Lucie Manette, later Darnay

Dickens describes Lucie as being beautiful physically and spiritually, and she possesses a gift for bringing out the best qualities of those around her. She is one of the lesser-developed characters in the novel, but she is "the golden thread" that binds many of the characters' lives together. A reader can best judge Lucie by her actions and influences on other characters rather than by her dialogue, which tends to be melodramatic and full of stock sentimentality. Her dialogue aside, Dickens portrays her as a compassionate, virtuous woman who inspires great love and loyalty in the other characters. For example, Darnay, Carton, and Stryver all court her and envision their futures being made brighter with her as their wife. Additionally, both Mr. Lorry and Miss Pross, who are without families, love Lucie as if she were their daughter and do everything they can to keep her safe. Although Lucie is a flat character, she is an important one. She represents unconditional love and compassion, and Dickens uses her to demonstrate how powerful these qualities can be, even in the face of violence and hatred.

Charles Darnay

Although Darnay rejects the Evrémonde name and inheritance and moves to England, he cannot escape his family history. Trying to make amends to an unknown woman whose family was wiped out by his father and uncle, he is arrested for treason in England; trying to save a jailed family servant, he is arrested in revolutionary France, where he is tried twice. His sense of responsibility motivates him to right wrongs, but he is otherwise a passive character who lets events direct his fate rather than trying to control it himself. Forces outside of his control inevitably foil even his attempts to assert himself and atone for his family's transgressions, placing him in increasingly dangerous situations from which he must be rescued.

Darnay represents justice and duty, qualities inherited from his mother. He (and his mother) also stands for the members of the French aristocracy who were aware of the damage their families were inflicting, but who could do nothing to prevent it. Darnay's willingness to atone for his family's wrongs and to work for a living demonstrate that eventually something good can come out of evil, a point that Dickens emphasizes at the end of the novel.

Sydney Carton

Carton, Darnay's double and alter-ego, has wasted his life on alcohol and apathy. He makes his intelligence obvious through his ability to analyze cases for Stryver. He makes clear that he had the same opportunities for success as Stryver, but for some reason chose not to take them. Besides some vague references to his student days and the disclosure that his parents died when he was young, Carton's past remains

a mystery to the reader. Consequently, the reader can only guess at wh...
caused him to become so dissolute. The only noble part of his life is h...
love for Lucie and his affection for the rest of her family. His love fo...
her is strong enough to induce him to give his life for that of her hu...
band. Carton takes on a mythical aspect in sacrificing himself to sav...
his friends. He represents the sacrificial hero who is ritually slaughtere...
of his own free will so that society might renew itself, a prospect he env...
sions before he dies. Through his death, he redeems his sins and...
reborn in the afterlife and through the life of his namesake.

Therese Defarge

Childless and merciless, Madame Defarge is the antithesis of Luci...
Manette. Both women possess the ability to inspire others, but whil...
Lucie creates and nurtures life, Madame Defarge destroys it. Becaus...
her entire family perished when she was a young girl, Madame Defarg...
wants revenge, not merely on the family that caused the evil but on th...
entire class from which it came. What makes her such a threatening fig...
ure is her stubborn patience, which bides its time until it can strike. I...
this she is like some natural force that, when the opportunity is righ...
becomes ferocious and unrelenting. Her secret management of Da...
nay's re-arrest is cunning, but shows immense cruelty as well. In seek...
ing to avenge her family, she has acquired the same ruthlessness as th...
men who destroyed her family. Her knitting represents both he...
patience and her urge to retaliate, because she knits the names of he...
intended victims. Symbolically, Madame Defarge stands for the inten...
sity and bloodthirst behind the Revolution. Her relentless drive fo...
vengeance makes her strong, but it eventually destroys her because sh...
is unable to comprehend the powerful love that gives Carton th...
strength to die for Darnay, and Miss Pross the courage to defeat her.

Ernest Defarge

Defarge was Doctor Manette's servant as a young man, and he seem...
to have a filial reverence for him during the Revolution. However, whe...
the Doctor was newly released from prison, Defarge was not abov...
exploiting his insanity as a spectacle to further the revolutionary caus...
As a revolutionary leader, Defarge organizes the Jacquerie and helps lea...
the mob in storming the Bastille. He bases his desire for revolution mor...
upon a desire for positive change than the bloodthirst of his wife, a...
demonstrated when he resists denouncing Doctor Manette, Lucie, an...

young Lucie simply because of their relationship to Darnay. His wife interprets his scruples as weakness, giving the reader the impression that before long revolutionaries such as Jacques Three will turn on Defarge and send him to the guillotine himself. Defarge represents the more rational aspect of the Revolution. He is not blinded by class hatred and retains his conscience and sense of fairness. His ability to empathize with those people Madame Defarge views as enemies, however, will probably result in his death, showing how out of control the Revolution became as paranoia and violence destroyed its positive forces.

Jerry Cruncher

A porter for Tellson's by day and a grave robber by night, he provides some of the little comedy in *A Tale of Two Cities*. His euphemisms create a topsy-turvy world in which grave robbing becomes respectable and prayer is degraded to "flopping." In digging up buried bodies, he parodies the theme of resurrection. Similarly, Jerry's scenes of wife abuse at home provide a darkly comedic contrast to the idyllic domestic scenes in Lucie's Soho home. He serves as a lever in the plot when his knowledge of Roger Cly's fake burial enables Carton to blackmail John Barsad effectively. In the end, Cruncher redeems himself when he renounces grave robbing and accepts his wife's piety.

CRITICAL ESSAYS

On the pages that follow, the writer of this study guide provides critical scholarship on various aspects of Dickens' *A Tale of Two Cities*. These interpretive essays are intended solely to enhance your understanding of the original literary work; they are supplemental materials and are not to replace your reading of *A Tale of Two Cities*. When you're finished reading *A Tale of Two Cities*, and prior to your reading this study guide's critical essays, consider making a bulleted list of what you think are the most important themes and symbols. Write a short paragraph under each bullet explaining why you think that theme or symbol is important; include at least one short quote from the original literary work that supports your contention. Then, test your list and reasons against those found in the following essays. Do you include themes and symbols that the study guide author doesn't? If so, this self test might indicate that you are well on your way to understanding original literary work. But if not, perhaps you will need to re-read *A Tale of Two Cities*.

Women in *A Tale of Two Cities* 102

The French Revolution 103

Women in *A Tale of Two Cities*

Curiously, one of the aspects readers most commonly overlook when studying *A Tale of Two Cities* is the centrality of women in the story. The characters around whom the action revolves in both London and Paris are women: Lucie Manette and Madame Defarge. Additionally, Dickens uses women throughout the book to represent the moral climate of a group or family. Although Dickens may not develop his female characters as fully as he does some of the male characters in *A Tale of Two Cities*, nevertheless, the women provide the men in the novel with an emotional foundation that causes the men to act for or react against what the women represent.

Lucie and Madame Defarge, for instance, drive the action in their respective spheres of influence. As the "golden thread" that binds the lives of Doctor Manette, Mr. Lorry, Darnay, and Carton together, Lucie is a passive character who influences others through who she is rather than by what she does. The comfortable home she creates comforts the men in her life and her devout compassion for others inspires them. Her goodness enables them to become more than they are and to find the strength to escape the prisons of their lives.

On the other hand, Madame Defarge stands at the center of the revolutionary activity in Paris as an active agent of change, even when she is just sitting in the wine-shop and knitting her death register. Madame Defarge instigates hatred and violence, exemplified by her leadership in the mob scenes and the way The Vengeance and Jacques Three feed off of her desire to exterminate the Evrémonde line. Her patient ruthlessness helps to support her husband when he has doubts about the Revolution. In the end, however, her desire for revenge becomes something Monsieur Defarge reacts against as he recognizes that the killing must end somewhere.

Dickens also portrays the other women in the novel as either nurturing life or destroying it. Mothers play an especially important role in this sense, as Dickens differentiates between natural and unnatural mothers. Women such as Darnay's mother, Madame Evrémonde, and Lucie's mother, Madame Manette, represented mothers who die young but leave their children with a sense of conscience and love. Madame Evrémonde's exhortations to Darnay to atone for the family's wrongdoing, for instance, motivate him to risk his life in order to help others. Lucie is also a natural mother, nurturing her daughter and protecting her from harm.

The women of Monseigneur's court, however, represent unnatural mothers, who care so little for their children that they push them off on wet nurses and nannies and pretend that the children don't even exist. Similarly, Dickens portrays even the mothers of Saint Antoine who do nurture their children as unnatural in the fact that they can spend the day as part of a vicious mob killing and beheading people and then return home smeared with blood to play with their children. The behaviors of both the aristocratic and the peasant women are destructive in that they either create an environment that lacks love and guidance or they guide the next generation into further anger and violence.

The French Revolution

When Louis XVI became King of France in 1775, he inherited a country with economic distress, social unrest, a debauched court, and problems with the nobility and *parlement* (the courts of justice). The inheritance was fatal. At the time, the aristocracy was living on borrowed money and the labors of the lower classes. The middle class was becoming wealthy from its trade, manufacturing, banking, and contracting. The lower middle class consisted of tradesmen and laborers, with a few government officials.

The king, only twenty, was inexperienced and easily influenced, and he soon tired of his country's problems. He was a shy man who was often indecisive and narrow-minded; he usually depended on his ministers for advice but frequently would reverse their decisions and decide matters for himself, simply because he wanted to show his authority. He sincerely believed that he ruled by the will of God, by the Divine Right of Kings.

The court was in debt and in dire need of money because of years of royal extravagance, financial deficits, and two wars. In order to cope with these problems, Louis reinstated the *parlements*, which were made up of aristocrats; he hoped that they could solve his problems. Although the lower classes were suffering, the magistrates in the *parlements* believed that reforms to help the lower classes were unnecessary. They thought that the lower classes needed no social reforms and that such people were born to bear the burdens of taxation. In contrast, members of the nobility, because of their birth into the upper class, or Second Estate, were exempt from *any* taxation. Not surprisingly, therefore, the *parlements* passed numerous laws favoring the aristocracy.

The *parlements* next asked Louis to return French rule to the Estates General (a body that had not met since 1614), and eventually Louis gave in. Three legal status groups, or Estates, comprised the Estates General—called simply, the First, Second, and Third Estates. In the First Estate were the clergy, usually the younger sons of the nobility. The Second Estate comprised the nobility, while the Third Estate included members of the working classes, plus some well-to-do merchants and professional men such as lawyers, doctors, and members of the minor clergy. Under the rule of the Estates-General, only the nobility could hold public office, high ranks in the military, important posts in the government, or sit in *parlements*.

The commoners of France, overjoyed when Louis established the Estates-General, soon became disappointed. Initially, they thought that they would have their "own" Estate and, thus, a voice in government policy-making. They quickly realized, however, that they possessed no real power. Organizing the new Estates-General on the same principle of the 1614 concept meant one vote for each member of the Estates. Thus, the clergy and the aristocracy could easily out-vote the Third Estate, two to one, which they did repeatedly.

Political problems increased, and food riots broke out due to food shortages. Rainstorms and hail ruined the crops of 1788, leaving people hungry. Paris, in particular, was a crowded, densely populated city of poor people. The masses had no jobs and no money. They began burning and looting the countryside, and even common soldiers began talking against their aristocratic officers. Political pamphlets aggravated the situation by demanding that the Third Estate have a stronger voice in the government.

By the middle of June 1788, poor parish priests who belonged to the First Estate began to desert their political base and join the Third Estate. As a result, the Third Estate recognized that it was the only Estate elected by "the people." They declared themselves "the National Assembly," and immediately banned taxes.

This declaration placed Louis in an uncomfortable and difficult position. Recognizing the legitimacy of the National Assembly would mean surrendering his power, but not recognizing it might drive the Third Estate to even greater rebellion. Unfortunately, he chose to listen to Jacques Necker, his Minister of Finance, and to his queen, Marie Antoinette, and decided to oppose the National Assembly. He closed the chambers where the Assembly was to convene, but the Assembly immediately moved to an indoor tennis court. Despite the confusion, the Assembly took an oath not to disband until they had a constitution, and they openly defied the king. They would have a constitution.

Three days later, Louis vetoed the legitimacy of the National Assembly and ordered the Estates-General to return to their traditional system or he would dismiss them. When he left, the Second and most of the First Estate followed him out. The Third Estate remained, and one of them, Mirabeau, shouted that the Third Estate would leave the assembly hall "only at the point of a bayonet!" Louis could not bring himself to use force against the Estate because so many clergymen and liberal noblemen had joined them. In a dramatic move, they defied the King and won. The Revolution had begun.

Paris, always a hotbed of dissension, had a large populace ready to fight against almost anything. In every corner, people seemed to meet and conspire; everywhere, people talked of revolution. Hunger haunted the city, and bread shortages constantly loomed over the population. Thieves often stole grain shipped into the city before it even arrived, and in the early summer of 1789, bread riots broke out.

Because the thousands of workers' salaries could not possibly keep pace with soaring prices, workers began wrecking factories and burning property. At this point, the Swiss Guard marched into Paris in early July. Rumors immediately spread that the aristocrats were going to try to stop the Revolution by armed force. In fact, however, Louis simply stationed the Swiss Guard where he did because the French Guard refused to fight against their own countrymen.

Four days before the Bastille fell, Louis dismissed Necker and the rest of his cabinet and appointed a new council of anti-revolutionary royalists. Almost immediately, rumors arose that the Swiss Guard and the German Guard were preparing to murder the Parisian populace. Even the French Guard believed the rumors. They joined the rioting masses and broke into the Tuileries Palace, taking gunpowder, ornamental guns, and a cannon. Rioting and looting continued, destroying small shops and government buildings.

On July 14, a mob of citizens seized 30,000 muskets from the Invalides and attacked the Bastille, where the French government kept the royal store of gunpowder. They hung and butchered the governor and his guards and released the few prisoners. Strangely enough, the mob still had sympathetic feelings for Louis; they had lost all respect for him as a king, but still felt affection for him.

In fact, the common people didn't fear Louis as much as they feared the cluster of noblemen surrounding him. Paranoia about royalist schemes to quash the Revolution overtook them, and so they looted and burned chateaus throughout the countryside. The people slaughtered landlords simply because they were landlords. Consequently, aristocrats began leaving France in droves; the country was no longer safe for anyone but a ragged revolutionary. These uprisings and the general climate were part and parcel of the "Great Fear."

On August 4, the National Assembly passed a measure invalidating all feudal rights of the aristocracy. The Assembly decided to divide France into 83 departments, giving considerable freedom to all the departments. Then they passed a law that, ironically, caused an even greater schism between the classes. The new law stated that anyone could vote—if they had paid their taxes. The peasants felt betrayed; they had no money to pay taxes. The aristocracy had already taxed them to death, and the Revolution was doing nothing for them.

The Assembly also suspended Louis from power until he signed the new constitution and accepted his role as only a "constitutional monarch." Robespierre denounced him, and the *sans-culottes*—a revolutionary group of small businessmen, laborers, and artisans, as well as the very poor—demanded his removal. In addition, they called for a Republic.

The new government began issuing paper money as legal tender because it associated gold with aristocrats and the wealthy. Exiled nobles, therefore, flooded France with forged paper money, adding to the already deflated money value. Food prices continued to rise, and even two years of good harvests failed to alleviate the peasants' hunger. Mobs began raiding and robbing supply convoys. Soap was in short supply and sugar was disappearing. Food riots began again.

Eventually, the National Assembly deposed Louis, put him and his family under arrest, and sent him to prison in the Knights Templars temple on August 13, 1792. The Assembly guillotined Louis on January 21, 1793. In August, the Assembly sent the queen to prison. It tried her in October and guillotined her on October 16, 1793.

Robespierre then took control of the Revolution, and the "Reign of Terror" began. He championed "the people's rights," but could not understand why the masses ranked food and better wages as more important than dedication to the principles of a free France. He saw conspirators and plotters everywhere, and anyone disagreeing with him became a traitor. He convinced his colleagues that the preservation of a safe society required force and terror. As a result, the new government executed hundreds at Marseilles and Toulon and drowned nearly two thousand in the Loire River at Nantes. The Revolutionary Tribunal was subdivided into four courts, which sat day and night. By September, the Law of Suspects had created so many accused people that the court tried cases in groups of fifty. Courts tried everyone: priests, hoarders, swindlers, aristocrats, and, of course, innocent men and women. Neighbor turned in neighbor. In all, the Tribunal killed more than twenty-five thousand people during the Reign of Terror.

The *sans-culottes* closed all the churches in Paris and even took over Notre-Dame cathedral and made it an atheistic "Temple of Reason." This decision upset Robespierre, but his followers equally disapproved of Robespierre's police bureau. They plotted Robespierre's downfall and eventually accused him—just as he had accused others—and sent him to the guillotine. After Robespierre's death, France moved into a period called the Thermidorian reaction, a relatively quiet period. The new government, called the Directory, was inefficient and corrupt, but provided a relatively stable regime nevertheless. Unfortunately, the new government put Napoleon Bonaparte in charge of its army. Unwittingly, it replaced the country's terrorists with someone who would soon become its virtual dictator.

CliffsNotes Review

Use this CliffsNotes Review to test your understanding of the original text, and reinforce what you've learned in this book. After you work through the review and essay questions, identify the quote section, and the fun and useful practice projects, you're well on your way to understanding a comprehensive and meaningful interpretation of Dickens' *A Tale of Two Cities.*

Q&A

1. Name the two cities to which the title refers?

2. Why does Dickens use the phrase "recalled to life" in reference to Doctor Manette?

3. How does Sydney Carton save Charles Darnay from being found guilty of treason during the trial in England?

4. During the day Jerry Cruncher is a porter for Tellson's Bank. What is his occupation at night?

5. What is Madame Defarge knitting?

6. Why does the Doctor spend nine days shoemaking after Lucie and Darnay get married?

7. Why does Darnay return to France in 1792?

8. What three people denounce Darnay when the revolutionaries arrest him for a second time in France?

9. How does Madame Defarge die?

10. How does Carton switch places with Darnay in prison?

Answers: (1) London and Paris. (2) Doctor Manette has been "buried alive" in prison for eighteen years. When he is released, or "recalled to life." Mr. Lorry travels to Paris to restore him to a normal life. (3) Carton points out the striking resemblance between Darnay and himself, which wrecks the credibility of a witness's testimony. (4) Jerry is a resurrection man, or a grave robber. He digs up fresh corpses to sell to a surgeon for dissection. (5) Madame Defarge is knitting a register of people who are enemies of the Revolution and who will be condemned to die when the revolutionaries take power. (6) The revelation that his new son-in-law is the son of the man who sent the Doctor to prison for eighteen years trau matizes him. (7) He returns to France to assist Gabelle, his family's stew ard, who is in prison for helping Darnay. (8) Monsieur and Madam Defarge and Doctor Manette denounce Darnay. The Doctor's denounce ment comes in the form of a letter he wrote in prison years earlie (9) While struggling with Miss Pross, Madame Defarge shoots herself wit her own gun. (10) He gains access to the prison through John Barsad, spy. Carton then changes clothes with Darnay, drugs him, and arrange for the guards to take Darnay out of the prison in his place.

Identify the Quote: Find Each Quote in *A Tale of Two Cities*

1. It was the best of times, it was the worst of times.

2. I have sometimes sat alone here of an evening, listening, until I have mad the echoes out to be the echoes of all the footsteps that are coming by and-by into our lives.

3. When the time comes, let loose a tiger and a devil; but wait for the tim with the tiger and the devil chained—not shown, yet always ready.

4. It is a far, far better thing that I do, than I have ever done; it is a far, fa better rest that I go to than I have ever known.

Answers: (1) Narrator; Book I, Chapter 1. (2) Lucie Manette; Book I Chapter 6. (3) Madame Defarge; Book II, Chapter 16. (4) Sydney Car ton; Book III, Chapter 15.

Essay Questions

1. Explain the first paragraph of the novel. What does Dickens mean by "I was the best of times, it was the worst of times"?

2. Discuss the resurrection theme in *A Tale of Two Cities*. Which character are "recalled to life"? How?

3. Describe how Dickens depicts crowds and mobs throughout the novel What does Dickens seem to be saying about large groups of people?

4. A major criticism of *A Tale of Two Cities* is that Dickens does not full develop his characters. Do you agree with this assessment? Explain wh or why not.

5. Discuss the use of light and shadow imagery throughout the novel.

6. Dickens represents women as being "natural" or "unnatural" in *A Tale of Two Cities*. What characteristics does he idealize in women? What characteristics does he view as abnormal? Do you agree or disagree with his perspective? Why?

7. Dickens is known for his humor, but *A Tale of Two Cities* is noticeably somber. Do any comic passages and characters exist in the novel? If so, what are they? Why are they humorous?

8. Discuss Dickens' views of the French Revolution. Does he believe it was inevitable or preventable? What are his attitudes toward the French royalty and aristocrats? Toward the peasants and revolutionaries?

Practice Projects

1. Construct a Web site that other students reading *A Tale of Two Cities* could use. The Web site could include a page about major themes in the book, a page about Charles Dickens, and a page about the French Revolution.

2. Write some journal entries from the perspective of one of the main characters.

3. Create a timeline that outlines the events of the novel and the events of the French Revolution.

CliffsNotes Resource Center

The learning doesn't need to stop here. The CliffsNotes Resource Center show
you the best of the best—links to the best information in print and online about th
author and/or related works. And don't think that this is all we've prepared for you
we've put all kinds of pertinent information at www.cliffsnotes.com. Loo
for all the terrific resources at your favorite bookstore or local library and on the Inte
net. When you're online, make your first stop www.cliffsnotes.com whe
you'll find more incredibly useful information about Dickens' *A Tale of Two Cities*

Books and Articles

This CliffsNotes book, published by Wiley Publishing, Inc., provides a meaningfu
interpretation of Dickens' *A Tale of Two Cities*. If you are looking for informatio
about the author and/or related works, check out these other publications:

ACKROYD, PETER. *Dickens*. New York: HarperCollins, 1990. Possibly the be
   biography of Dickens ever written, Ackroyd skillfully details Dickens' life i
   an engaging narrative style that will transport you back to Victorian Englan
   and make you eager to read all of Dickens' works.

DAVIS, PAUL. Charles Dickens A to Z. New York: Checkmark, 1998. An exce
   lent resource for students, teachers, and general readers. With 2,500 entries o
   Dickens' life and works, this book provides historical background material tha
   will enrich a reader's understanding of any Dickens novel.

GLANCY, RUTH. *A Tale of Two Cities: Dickens's Revolutionary Novel*. Bostor
   Twayne, 1991. The author provides a thorough discussion of the novel an
   explains the importance of *A Tale of Two Cities* and its critical reception. Add
   tionally, the author gives the novel a careful reading and examines the signif
   cance of main characters and patterns of imagery.

NEWLIN, GEORGE. *Understanding a Tale of Two Cities*. Westport, CT: Greer
   wood, 1998. This book is important for anyone serious about learning mor
   about the historical context of *A Tale of Two Cities*. It includes a chronology o
   the historical and fictitious events in the novel and also contains many of th
   original sources that Dickens used in writing the book.

SCHAMA, SIMON. *Citizens: A Chronicle of the French Revolution*. New York: Vir
   tage, 1989. An exceptional history of the French Revolution, it presents th
   facts of the revolution in a compelling narrative that conveys both the terrc
   and the excitement of the dramatic period.

CHLICKE, PAUL, ed. *Oxford Reader's Companion to Dickens*. Oxford: Oxford UP, 1999. A thorough reference on Dickens and his works, this book provides detailed entries on all of Dickens' characters and works, as well as in-depth discussions of Dickens' public and private life and the people and events that influenced him.

's easy to find books published by Wiley Publishing, Inc. You'll find them in your avorite bookstores, on the Internet, and at a store near you. We also have three web tes that you can use to read about all the books we publish:

- www.cliffsnotes.com

- www.dummies.com

- www.wiley.com

nternet

Check out these Web resources for more information about Charles Dickens, *A Tale f Two Cities,* and Dickens' other works:

Charles Dickens." http://www.helsinki.fi/kasv/nokol/dickens.html. This site provides extensive links to Dickens-related sites, including full-text versions of Dickens' books and Dickens' speeches. It offers some good historical information that can't be found elsewhere.

Charles Dickens Gad's Hill Place." http://www.perryweb.com/ Dickens/. A fun site to browse, it has some interesting pictures, a fairly good Dickens biography, and most importantly, a quote search. The quote search might be a helpful tool for instructors teaching a Dickens book or for students writing a paper on a Dickens book.

The Dickens Project." http://humwww.ucsc.edu/dickens/index.html. This is the Web site for the University of California's center for Dickens studies. Because of its affiliation with a university, it has a more scholarly bent and is a good place to start if you're interested in doing some more serious work on Dickens and his works. It provides updates on academic conferences and research, has a Dickens electronic archive, and provides links to other online resources.

Rochester Dickens Fellowship." http://members.tripod.com/ DickensFellowship CD/. This is the official Web site of one of the founding branches of the Dickens Fellowship—an organization devoted to celebrating Dickens. Its illustrations and regional information make it worthwhile to visit, especially to get a taste of how the English celebrate Dickens.

"The Victorian Web." `http://landow.stg.brown.edu/victorian` `victov.html`. A phenomenal collection of information and links abou everything and anything you might need to know about the Victorian era, th site includes history, religion, gender matters, technology, economics, the visu arts, and more.

Recordings

BBC Radio Presents A Tale of Two Cities. New York: Bantam, 1988. A great drama tization of *A Tale of Two Cities*, the lively characterizations and faithful repr duction of Dickens' language and tone make this production an excelle learning aid and supplement to the text.

ndex

A

Tale of Two Cities: Dickens Revolutionary
  Novel (Glancy), 112
ckroyd, Peter, 112
ll the Year Round, 7
istocracy, extravagances of French, 42
m-chest, 21

B

ank note, 31
arnaby Rudge, 4
arsad, John, 13, 34, 55. See also Pross,
  Solomon
ase nature of people
  coutroom scene depicting, 32
astille, storming of, 63
BC Radio Presents: A Tale of Two Cities
  (recording), 114
eadnell, Maria, 2
ear leader, 52
edlam, 33
leak House, 4
ooks and articles, list of, 112, 113
ritish legal system,condemnation of, 32
uried alive theme, 68, 69

C

arlyle, Thomas, 7
arton, Sydney, 12
  asks Darnay's friendship, 61
  character analysis, 97
  character insight, 36, 38
  complexities of, 34
  Darnay as mirror image of, 36
  farewell scene, strength during, 85
  imprisonment, self-inflicted, 50
  rescue of Darnay, 34
  Styver compared to, 38
aracter analysis
  Charles Darnay, 97
  Doctor Alexandre Manette, 96
  Ernest Defarge, 98

  Jerry Cruncher, 99
  Lucie Manette, 96
  Sydney Carton, 97
  Therese Defarge, 98
character insight
  Charles Darnay, 36, 61
  Doctor Manette, 59, 60
  Ernest Defarge, 53
  Jarvis Lorry, 24
  Lucie Manette, 40
  Sydney Carton, 36, 38
  Therese Defarge, 27, 34, 53
characters, list of, 12–14
Charles Dickens (Web site), 113
Charles Dickens A to Z (Davis), 112
"Charles Dickens Gad's Hill Place," 113
Citizens: A Chronicle of the French Revolution
  (Schama), 113
claret, 25
climax of book, Doctor Manette's
  secret as, 84
Cly, Roger, 13
  funeral, 51
  witness against Darnay, 34
coach and six, 23
Cock-lane ghost, 18
Collins, Wilkie, 7
critics, 9
crowds, basest nature of people and, 32
Cruncher, Jerry, 13
  character analysis, 99
  fired from Tellson's, 81
  resurrection and, 52
  secrets, having, 30, 31
Cruncher, Mrs., 13, 30
Cruncher, Young Jerry, 13, 30, 51
cutlass, 21

D

Darnay, Charles, 12
  Carton as mirror image of, 36
  character analysis, 97
  character insight, 36, 61
  fairness and justice, embodiment of
    belief in, 46
  first sight of Lucie, 32
  imprisoned at La Force, 69
  inability to see real Carton, 61
  rejection of uncle and country, 46
  returns to France to save Gabelle, 68

Darnay, Lucie
   See Manette, Lucie, 12
Darnay, Young Lucie, 14
Davis, Paul, 112
Death, farmer personified as, 93
dechristianization movement, allusion to, 74
Defarge, Ernest, 13
   character analysis, 98
   fairness and justice aspect of
      rebellion in, 53
   life and death, views on, 56
   moral differences with wife, 55
   Revolution, embodiment of ideas and
      emotions of, 27
Defarge, Therese, 13
   character analysis, 98
   character insight, 27, 34
   death of, 91
   life and death, views on, 56
   Lucie Manette as opposite of, 72
   moral differences with husband, 55
   as representative of evil, 102
   revenge and death aspect of
      rebellion in, 53
   Revolution, embodiment of ideas and
      emotions of, 27
   ruthlessness of, 65, 78
   secret of childhood trauma revealed,
      87, 88
   unnatural woman, as, 73
Dickens (Ackroyd), 112
Dickens, Charles
   career highlights, 3
   death of, 3
   early years, 2
   education of, 2
   employment of, 2
   estranged from wife, 2
   marriage of, 2
"Dickens Project," 113
Dombey and Son, 4
doubles and mirror images
   Carton and Darnay as, 36, 89
   Evremonde brothers, 84
   Lucie and Madame Defarge as, 72
drawer, 25
duality theme, 17

E

emotional center of novel, Lucie
   Manette as, 40
escutcheon, 43

F

farmer, Death personified as, 93
farrier, 70
film interpretations, 9
finger post, 43
flambeau, 45
flint and steel, 21
Foulon, 14, 64
French Revolution, 103–107
French Revolution, The, 7
Frozen Deep, The, 7
funeral procession, crowd turning into
   destructive mob during, 51

G

Gabelle, Theophile, 14, 44, 66, 67
gaols, 19
Gaspard, 14, 42, 53
Glancy, Ruth, 112
good, evil overcome by, 92
Great Expectations, 4

H

hackney coach, 31
hate, forces of love versus forces of, 74, 92
highwayman, 19
historical events, fictionalization of , 63, 64
Hogarth, Catherine, 7

I

ideal woman, Lucie Manette as, 41, 72
imagery
   setting sun as blood, 44
   use of, 9
   wine as blood, 26

J

jackal, 39
jack-boots, 21
Jacques One, Two, Three, and Four, 14, 26,
   53, 64, 81, 87, 91

L

language and style
   death, Tellson's Bank in business of, 30
   Defarges used to embody ideas and
      emotions of Revolution, 27

violence, prediction of future, 26
wine symbolizing blood, 26
ludanum, 31
erary device
circular feel of novel, 69
conflict between love and hate, 92
French aristocracy and lower class,
representation of relationship
between, 88
ideal woman, Lucie as, 41, 72
light and dark, 28
secrecy, 22
ttle Dorrit, 4
rry, Jarvis, 13
character insight, 24
as link between France and England, 20
physical details revealed, 24, 25
ve, forces of hate versus forces of, 74, 92

M

anette, Doctor Alexandre, 12
character analysis, 96
character, depth of, 59, 60
character insight, 59, 60
influence with revolutionaries, 11, 71
revelation of secret as climax of book, 84
anette, Lucie, 12
character analysis, 96
character insight, 40
courage of, 76
as emotional center of novel, 40
as ideal woman, 41
Madame Defarge as opposite of, 72
as representative of good, 102
wedding of, 58
artin Chuzzlewit, 4
elodrama
farewell scene between Darnay and
Lucie, 85
reunion scene between Lucie and her
father, 29
irror images. See doubles and mirror images
ob
behavior of, 71
Doctor Manette's influence on mob
violence, 71
transformation of people in a, 64
women becoming, 63
oral climate, women as
representatives of, 102

mystery and secrecy, 8, 81
imprisonment of Dr. Manette, 40
Mr. Lorry's business, 20
Mystery of Edwin Drood, 5

N

Newlin, George, 112
Nicholas Nickleby, 3

O

Old Curiosity Shop, The, 3
online resources, 112, 113
opposites. See doubles and mirror images
Oxford Reader's Companion to Dickens
(Schlicke), 113

P

packet, 25
personal board, 31
Pickwick Papers, The, 3
pier glass, 25
pikes, 63
pillory, 33
plot
character development and, 8
Doctor Manette's secret as climax of
book, 84
Jerry Cruncher and, 99
Lucie's character and, 76
Therese Defarge's secret revealed, 87
unrelated minor plots coming
together, 79
Pross, Miss, 13
role as protector, 91
Pross, Solomon, 13, 79. See also Barsad, John
provender, 29
public house, 52
publications, list of, 112, 113
purloiner, 31

R

recordings (audio), 114
Reign of Terror, 74, 106
resurrection man, 52
resurrection theme, 9, 64, 68
Carton and, 81, 89, 94
Darnay's resurrection, 34, 77
Jerry Cruncher and, 52

revolution
  danger of, 8
  as force of nature , 66
road-mender, 14, 44, 53. *See also* wood-sawyer
robing room, 37
Rochester Dickens Fellowship, 114

S

sacristan, 66
Samson, literary significance of, 75
Schama, Simon, 113
Schlicke, Paul, 113
seamstress, 14
secret selves theme, 81
serial literature, popularity of, 3
shroud, 54
smelling salts, 25
Southcott, Joanna, 18
St. Evremonde, Marquis, 13, 14, 44
  Darnay's rejection of, 46
  death of, 46
  unnaturalness of, 44
Stryver, C.J., 13, 38, 48
synopsis, 10, 11, 12

T

Tellson's Bank, run on, 62
Ternan, Ellen, 3, 7
theatrical interpretations, 9
themes
  basest nature of people, crowds bringing
    out, 32
  buried alive, being, 68, 69
  doubles and mirror images, 36, 89
  duality, 17
  mystery and secrecy, 8, 20, 40, 81
  resurrection, 9, 22, 34, 64, 68, 77, 81,
    89, 94
  secrecy and upheaval, 8
  secret selves, 81
tocsin, 66
turnkey, 19

U

Understanding a Tale of Two Cities
  (Newlin), 112
upper class, unnaturalness of French, 42, 44

V

vengeance
  Doctor Manette overcoming need for, 5
  Therese Defarge's desire for, 57, 73
Vengeance, The, 14, 64, 72, 87, 91
Victorian view of marriage, 48
"Victorian Web," 114
violence, escalation of, 53

W

Web sites, 113
  "Charles Dickens," 113
  "Charles Dickens Gad's Hill Place," 113
  "Dickens Project," 113
  Rochester Dickens Fellowship, 114
  "Victorian Web," 114
wicket, 70
winding sheet, 37
women
  centrality of, 102, 103
  life destroying, 103
  life nurturing, 102
  Lucie Manette as representative of
    good, 102
  mob, becoming a, 63
  morale climate, as representatives of, 102
  Therese Defarge as representative
    of evil, 102
wood-sawyer, 14, 76. *See also* road-mender

Y

Year One of Liberty, 75

NOTES

NOTES

lotes

TURE

Absalom!
id
non
Vonderland
ng's Men
etty Horses
on the
rn Front
&
Wives
Poets of the
Century
Tragedy
arm
enina
nd Cleopatra
Ethics
Dying
stant
ike It
ugged
graphy of
ranklin
graphy of
lm X
kening

& Benito
o
Trees

Jar

e
d & Typee
y
e Me
ouse
, Ultima
st Eye & Sula
ew World
hers Karamazov

The Call of the Wild & White Fang
Candide
The Canterbury Tales
Catch-22
Catcher in the Rye
The Chosen
The Color Purple
Comedy of Errors...
Connecticut Yankee
The Contender
The Count of Monte Cristo
Crime and Punishment
The Crucible
Cry, the Beloved Country
Cyrano de Bergerac
Daisy Miller & Turn...Screw
David Copperfield
Death of a Salesman
The Deerslayer
Diary of Anne Frank
Divine Comedy-I. Inferno
Divine Comedy-II. Purgatorio
Divine Comedy-III. Paradiso
Doctor Faustus
Dr. Jekyll and Mr. Hyde
Don Juan
Don Quixote
Dracula
Electra & Medea
Emerson's Essays
Emily Dickinson Poems
Emma
Ethan Frome
The Faerie Queene
Fahrenheit 451
Far from the Madding Crowd
A Farewell to Arms
Farewell to Manzanar
Fathers and Sons
Faulkner's Short Stories

Faust Pt. I & Pt. II
The Federalist
Flowers for Algernon
For Whom the Bell Tolls
The Fountainhead
Frankenstein
The French Lieutenant's Woman
The Giver
Glass Menagerie & Streetcar
Go Down, Moses
The Good Earth
The Grapes of Wrath
Great Expectations
The Great Gatsby
Greek Classics
Gulliver's Travels
Hamlet
The Handmaid's Tale
Hard Times
Heart of Darkness & Secret Sharer
Hemingway's Short Stories
Henry IV Part 1
Henry IV Part 2
Henry V
House Made of Dawn
The House of the Seven Gables
Huckleberry Finn
I Know Why the Caged Bird Sings
Ibsen's Plays I
Ibsen's Plays II
The Idiot
Idylls of the King
The Iliad
Incidents in the Life of a Slave Girl
Inherit the Wind
Invisible Man
Ivanhoe
Jane Eyre
Joseph Andrews
The Joy Luck Club
Jude the Obscure

Julius Caesar
The Jungle
Kafka's Short Stories
Keats & Shelley
The Killer Angels
King Lear
The Kitchen God's Wife
The Last of the Mohicans
Le Morte d'Arthur
Leaves of Grass
Les Miserables
A Lesson Before Dying
Light in August
The Light in the Forest
Lord Jim
Lord of the Flies
The Lord of the Rings
Lost Horizon
Lysistrata & Other Comedies
Macbeth
Madame Bovary
Main Street
The Mayor of Casterbridge
Measure for Measure
The Merchant of Venice
Middlemarch
A Midsummer Night's Dream
The Mill on the Floss
Moby-Dick
Moll Flanders
Mrs. Dalloway
Much Ado About Nothing
My Ántonia
Mythology
Narr. ...Frederick Douglass
Native Son
New Testament
Night
1984
Notes from the Underground

The Odyssey
Oedipus Trilogy
Of Human Bondage
Of Mice and Men
The Old Man and
    the Sea
Old Testament
Oliver Twist
The Once and
    Future King
One Day in the Life of
    Ivan Denisovich
One Flew Over the
    Cuckoo's Nest
100 Years of Solitude
O'Neill's Plays
Othello
Our Town
The Outsiders
The Ox Bow Incident
Paradise Lost
A Passage to India
The Pearl
The Pickwick Papers
The Picture of
    Dorian Gray
Pilgrim's Progress
The Plague
Plato's Euthyphro…
Plato's The Republic
Poe's Short Stories
A Portrait of the
    Artist…
The Portrait of a Lady
The Power and
    the Glory
Pride and Prejudice
The Prince
The Prince and
    the Pauper
A Raisin in the Sun
The Red Badge of
    Courage
The Red Pony
The Return of the
    Native
Richard II

Richard III
The Rise of
    Silas Lapham
Robinson Crusoe
Roman Classics
Romeo and Juliet
The Scarlet Letter
A Separate Peace
Shakespeare's
    Comedies
Shakespeare's Histories
Shakespeare's
    Minor Plays
Shakespeare's Sonnets
Shakespeare's Tragedies
Shaw's Pygmalion &
    Arms…
Silas Marner
Sir Gawain…Green
    Knight
Sister Carrie
Slaughterhouse-five
Snow Falling on Cedars
Song of Solomon
Sons and Lovers
The Sound and the Fury
Steppenwolf &
    Siddhartha
The Stranger
The Sun Also Rises
T.S. Eliot's Poems &
    Plays
A Tale of Two Cities
The Taming of the
    Shrew
Tartuffe, Misanthrope…
The Tempest
Tender Is the Night
Tess of the D'Urbervilles
Their Eyes Were
    Watching God
Things Fall Apart
The Three Musketeers
To Kill a Mockingbird
Tom Jones
Tom Sawyer
Treasure Island &

Kidnapped
The Trial
Tristram Shandy
Troilus and Cressida
Twelfth Night
Ulysses
Uncle Tom's Cabin
The Unvanquished
Utopia
Vanity Fair
Vonnegut's Works
Waiting for Godot
Walden
Walden Two
War and Peace
Who's Afraid of
    Virginia…
Winesburg, Ohio
The Winter's Tale
The Woman Warrior
Worldly Philosophers
Wuthering Heights
A Yellow Raft in
    Blue Water

Check Out the All-New CliffsNotes Guides

TECHNOLOGY TOPICS

Balancing Your Check-
    book with Quicken
Buying and Selling
    on eBay
Buying Your First PC
Creating a Winning
    PowerPoint 2000
    Presentation
Creating Web Pages
    with HTML
Creating Your First
    Web Page
Exploring the World
    with Yahoo!
Getting on the Internet

Going Online wi
Making Window
    Work for You
Setting Up a
    Windows 98
    Home Netwo
Shopping Online
Upgrading and
    Repairing You
Using Your First
Using Your First
Writing Your Firs
    Computer Pr

PERSONAL FINANCE TO

Budgeting & Sav
    Your Money
Getting a Loan
Getting Out of D
Investing for the
    First Time
Investing in
    401(k) Plans
Investing in IRAs
Investing in
    Mutual Funds
Investing in the
    Stock Market
Managing Your
Planning Your
    Retirement
Understanding
    Health Insura
Understanding
    Life Insurance

CAREER TOPI

Delivering a Win
    Job Interview
Finding a Job
    on the Web
Getting a Job
Writing a Great R